THE
COUNTRY
NORTH-
WARD

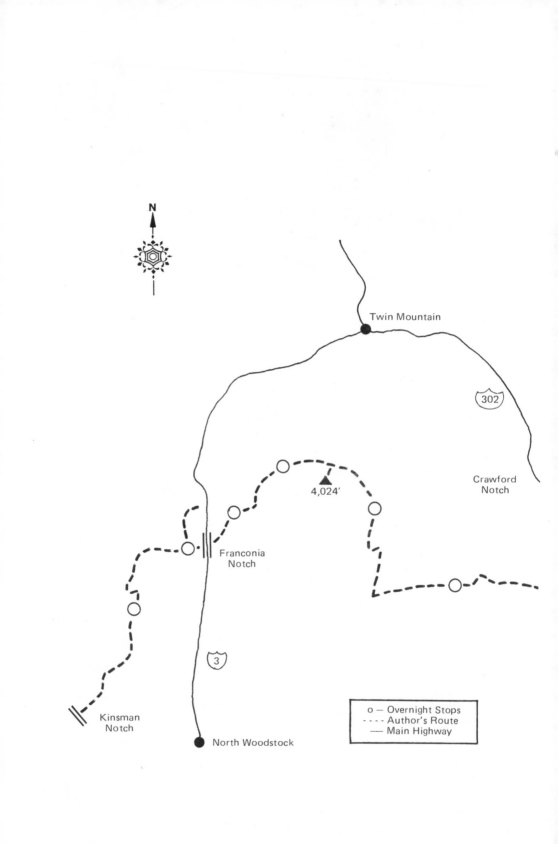

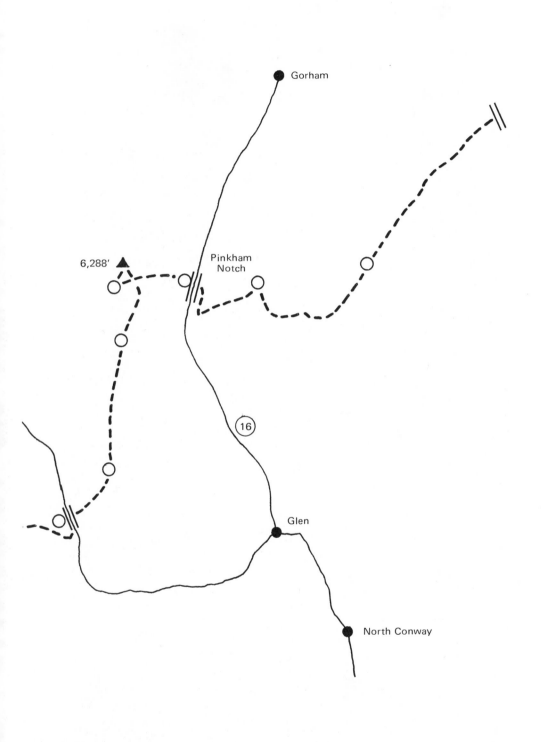

Gorham

6,288'

Pinkham
Notch

16

Glen

North Conway

THE COUNTRY NORTH- WARD

With photographs by the author

New Hampshire Publishing Company
Somersworth
1976

DANIEL FORD

Novels by Daniel Ford

NOW COMES THEODORA

INCIDENT AT MUC WA

THE HIGH COUNTRY ILLUMINATOR

Library of Congress Catalog Card Number 76-11306
International Standard Book Number 0-912274-60-3

New Hampshire Publishing Company, Somersworth

© 1976 by Daniel Ford
All rights reserved

In different form, much of chapter eight appeared in
Country Journal as "Thoughts on Peak Bagging," October
1975. © 1975 by Country Journal Publishing Co., Inc.
Permission to adapt this material is gratefully
acknowledged.

Designed by David Sykes

Printed in the United States of America

*The country beyond these hills northward
is daunting terrible, being full of rocky hills,
as thick as mole-hills in a meadow,
and cloathed with infinite thick woods.*

John Josselyn, 1672

Contents

for Sally, of course

Finding lost river

"You'll be sure to eat enough?" Sally said. "And you'll quit if the weather turns bad?"

"Of course."

"Otherwise I'll meet you at Crawford Notch on Sunday. . . . But what if you're late?"

"I won't be late."

"But what if you are?"

"If I'm behind schedule, I'll take a more direct route. Don't worry. I'll be there Sunday afternoon."

"But what if you break a leg or something?"

"Then I'll send a message out."

"All right," she said, not entirely convinced that she would ever see her husband again.

I don't mind suffering—in moderation, of course, and under circumstances of my own choosing—but Sally minds it a great deal. She doesn't even like to go without a bath for more than twenty-four hours at a stretch. So she wasn't tempted to walk across the White Mountains in my company. On the other hand, neither was she reconciled to the idea of sending her husband off to the wilderness alone. In vain I assured her that New Hampshire was wilderness no longer, and that my largest problem would not be the lack of companionship but finding room to sleep. The White Mountain National Forest is an exceedingly busy place in the summer and fall. In the good old days I'd walked almost every part of the New Hampshire mountains, always knowing that at nightfall I would find a roof over my head, in one of the three-sided shelters maintained by the U.S. Forest Service or the Appalachian Mountain Club. Then, about 1965, "backpacking" became one of the favored recreations of the young. As the trails grew crowded and the shelters jammed, I shifted to the winter months. I escalated my zone of discomfort, you might say. If you are willing to suffer more than the next person—if you are willing to wake up in the morning with snow in your face—you can still find solitude in this part of the country, though it is by no means guaranteed. Ski-touring and snowmobiling have also grown apace since 1965.

Still I was curious about the brave new world of the backpacker. So I freed myself of other obligations for two weeks of July, and I plotted a course that would take me clear across the White Mountain National Forest, both to its busiest and to its loneliest regions. I would walk from west to east, from Kinsman Notch to Hastings Plantation. The first is solidly in New Hampshire, about twenty miles from the Vermont border. The second is in Maine, although just barely. As I had planned my route, and with due allowance for side-trips here and there, the distance was exactly one hundred miles. Sally would meet me halfway, at Crawford Notch, where I would scrub myself and replenish my stores. It was this rendezvous that was worrying her at the moment. Today was Monday. I would have one chance to telephone her, when I passed through Franconia Notch on Wednesday, but then I would be out of touch until we met again on Sunday.

We were driving north on Interstate 93, the expressway that follows the Pemigewasset River to the mountains. Thanks to I-93, a Bostonian can now reach the foothills in less than two hours. In 1725, Capt. Samuel Willard led a "ranging company" from Massachusetts to the northern wilderness. The militiamen required nearly a month to march the present route of I-93, through Manchester, Concord, Plymouth, and North Woodstock.

"I wish I were going with you," Sally said.

"Really?"

"No, not really. But I'd like to *remember* it with you."

"Well, I'll keep a journal for you to read."

"Yes, do."

"Maybe I'll even write a book about it."

"If you do," Sally told me, "you'll have to dedicate it to—"

" 'To Sally'," I promised. "Of course."

"That's more like it," she said.

The interstate is a fine introduction to the mountains. It is not one highway but two: northbound and southbound, each road follows its own best route through the foothills. The median strip is half a mile wide in places. Today, as we drove past Plymouth at sixty miles an hour, we were separated from the southbound traffic by a broad scarf of yellow and purple—buttercups and clover in bloom.

The men who build these roads are a special breed, like the Jesuits. They are a kind of latter-day church, in fact, supported by a tax on the faithful who drive automobiles. (In New Hampshire the sanctity of the gasoline tax has been guaranteed by constitutional amendment. It can be used for no other purpose than to improve the roads.) The highwaymen spread asphalt the way the Jesuits used to spread the faith, building highways wherever we might care to go and some places we'd rather not. They will continue to build, as their critics like to say, until the last bulldozer runs out of gas.

In recent years there was great argument about extending I-93 through Franconia Notch, home of the Old Man of the Mountains. The abuse was richly deserved by the highwaymen, who designed and built the interstate in two distinct sections, closing upon the Old Man from north and south. Nobody took alarm until the southern leg reached Plymouth, and the lawsuits did not begin until it was open as far as North Woodstock. By that time a five-year-old with a ruler and a sense of proportion could have foretold that I-93 would be pushed through Franconia Notch, thus joining the northern and southern segments. At the moment the whole affair was tied up in the courts. One side argued that I-93 was essential to the economy of northern New Hampshire, the other that it would destroy the beauty of Franconia Notch.

To me, it didn't seem to matter very much. The importance of I-93 was not the Franconia Notch segment but the miles that had already been completed. Whether or not the Old Man of the Mountains ever looked down upon I-93, nothing could alter the fact that it already reached to his front gate, putting him within easy reach of the megalopolis to the south.

A classic dilemma. I-93 is a handsome road, and it offers quick passage from the city to the mountains; best of all, it has abolished the dreary gauntlet of billboards and motels that used to welcome the

13

northbound traveler. But while solving the old problems, I-93 has created a new one, as solutions have a way of doing. When the solution is an expressway, the new problem is that more people will choose to travel in whatever direction the expressway is going—in this case, to the White Mountains of New Hampshire.

We left the interstate at Exit 32, otherwise known as the town of North Woodstock. A country road took us west toward Kinsman Notch. Some tourists use this road, but not many; the enterprises are therefore limited to an Italian restaurant, some overnight cabins, and a second-home development or two. The signs were owner-painted. It was as if we had turned onto one of the back roads of my boyhood, when a Komfy Kabin could be rented for two dollars a night. There was also a billboard urging us to FIND LOST RIVER, which we soon did. Lost River is the main tourist attraction in Kinsman Notch; it belongs to the Society for the Protection of New Hampshire Forests, so it is about as inoffensive as a tourist attraction can be. Nothing is visible from the road except a parking lot and a small arrow pointing to "all activities."

We joined a dozen other cars in the parking lot, most of them from Massachusetts, but with delegates also from Connecticut, New Hampshire, and Quebec. We followed the arrow. It directed us to a natural-history display, a nature trail which would have taken us *away* from the concession, and a large sign quoting from Henry David Thoreau:

> I long for wildness . . .
> woods where the woodthrush forever sings,
> where the hours are early morning ones,
> and there is dew on the grass,
> and the day is forever unproven . . .
> a New Hampshire everlasting and unfallen.

*Though
halted for the
moment by
Federal court
action, Inter-
state 93 still
has its sights
on Franconia
Notch*

My sentiments exactly. To reinforce the argument, the north wall of Kinsman Notch loomed over us, looking as though it would never fall. I would be topping that rise in less than an hour.

Only after absorbing these sights were we allowed to spend any money at the Lost River concession. (The river isn't really lost; it just goes underground for a space, in caverns created by the glaciers that once passed this way.) We went into the restaurant, where I hoped to find the directions I needed. "You should have something to eat while you're here," Sally told me.

"Just a cup of coffee," I said.

She put a slab of chocolate cake on the tray. "You're not going up *that mountain* on an empty stomach," she said. She was right as always: the cake wasn't bad, while the coffee was dreadful.

I asked one of the guides where I might find the Kinsman Ridge Trail. The guides at Lost River are uniformed in jeans, plaid shirts, and red suspenders. Like those at Disneyland and all such places,

they are college students for the most part, young men and women who have the wit to memorize a few facts and the personality to relate the information to tourists. Unfortunately, the location of Kinsman Ridge Trail was not part of the regulation patter. So I tried the girl at the cash register. She looked to be a native of these parts.

"No," she said. "I never heard of—what did you call it?"

"The Kinsman Ridge Trail."

"Well, I never heard of that, but the Appalachian Trail goes across the road near here."

"That's what I want," I said.

"Oh," she said. "Well, go down the road for about half a mile, and you'll see a green sign. That's the Appalachian Trail," she added, with a certain emphasis on the name. If I wanted the AT, why hadn't I asked for it?

We returned to the parking lot in time to meet a young man in red suspenders, strolling towards us with a sheaf of bumper stickers in his hand. He gave us an apologetic smile. One of his advertisements was now attached to the front bumper of our little station wagon: I FOUND LOST RIVER. When Sally drove home along the interstate, she would be a billboard in her own right.

Half a mile to the west, as the cashier had promised, we saw the green-and-white sign that marked the crossing of the Appalachian Trail. It was a metal job, placed there by the highway department for the instruction of the tourists. The real marker was visible only after we had stopped. It was made of wood, and the letters—Kinsman Ridge Trail—had been cut into it by hand. Just beyond, the trail mounted steeply through the hardwoods. I unlocked the back of the car and took out my pack and walking stick.

"Aren't you *thrilled*?" Sally said.

"Yes I am."

"Do you have everything?"

"I hope so."

"Well. . . ." We kissed, and I started up the trail. "Have a wonderful time," Sally called after me. Then she added, "You look just like Thoreau!"

I don't know about that, but I am sure of one thing. Not even Thoreau could have entered the woods with more pleasure than I was feeling.

The appalachian trail ii

If there is a footpath more famous than the Appalachian Trail, more trodden and written about, I can't imagine what it might be. The latest chronicle comes in two volumes for $16.95. They contain "the absorbing stories of 46 men and women who have hiked the entire 2,023 miles of the Appalachian Trail from Maine to Georgia —the day-to-day adventures, hardships and satisfactions . . . 131 photographs in color." I won't attempt to compete with that, except to point out that the AT is usually hiked in the other direction, from Georgia to Maine, for reasons having to do with the weather and the black-fly population; and that many more than forty-six hikers have gone the whole distance. In 1973 alone, more than ninety men and women completed that long march.

In the White Mountains, the AT jogs along most of the high ridges, sometimes doubling back to ensure that the hikers experience the best New Hampshire has to offer. Most of these ridges were traveled long before the Appalachian Trail was conceived in 1921. Thus the trail in these parts is an overlay upon the older system, including the first eleven miles of the Kinsman Ridge Trail.

The first half-mile was a steep climb through birch and other hardwoods. Each step of the way was a flat rock, two or three hundred pounds muscled into place, so that climbing from Kinsman Notch was like climbing the steps of the Great Pyramid. Somebody had gone to a great deal of effort to pave my entry into the national forest.

While I was resting on one of these steps, catching my breath and generally melting into the mountain experience, I was startled by an automobile horn. One of the astonishing features of mountain walking is how quickly civilization drops behind. In the summer, in the hardwood forest, a few hundred yards is enough to smother the sound of a passenger car. Trucks are more bothersome, and motorcycles more bothersome still, but even they can be left behind in fifteen minutes of walking. The wilderness is that close to the highway.

But there was that foolish horn, blatting its foolish message. Then I recognized it as Sally's goodbye. She had made the turnaround and now was returning to the interstate—to home, family, and earning the odd dollar—while I went walking through the mountains. She was a good sport to tolerate that, and I saluted her with my walking stick. Thank you, Sally. I love you too.

The trail continued to amaze me. Not only were the ascents stepped with granite slabs, but the flat places were ditched like a country road of twenty-five years ago, a deep trench on either side to keep the middle dry. Where the ground was too low for ditching, it was bridged with logs sliced lengthwise by a chainsaw. That was another surprise, because the Appalachian Mountain Club was supposed to have a rule against power tools in the wilderness. Round logs were therefore the custom on trails—like this one—that were maintained by the AMC. Oh, if a route was especially popular with the sweatshirt-and-sneaker brigade, the trail crew might notch the logs with a two-man saw, then chip out the wood between the notches. That provided more traction for sneakers and street shoes. But a real hiker was expected to keep his footing on the basic log, however round and slippery.

Not here. The logs had been neatly halved, laid two or three wide, and spiked to crossties. The chainsaw wounds were still fresh. As

much as I had hiked in the White Mountains, I had never met a
logging crew, though logging is a continual and very big business in
the national forest. And I had never met a trail crew, though their
labors are also continuous. I amused myself, hiking along, with the
fancy that an AMC crew was working just beyond me. They had
posted a lookout to warn them of my approach, so they could hide in
the forest until I went by, not to spoil my enjoyment of the
wilderness.

Half an hour from the highway, I met two lads who were bound for
Kinsman Notch and who had spent last night at Eliza Brook Shelter.
The shelter was my destination, and a principal reason why I was in a
hurry. I favor a light pack, which among other things means that I
don't carry a proper tent—just a polyethylene tube and fifty feet of
parachute cord, so that I can rig a raincover in an emergency. Apart
from their weight, I don't like tents. They are brilliantly contrived, to
keep out the weather while weighing no more than six or seven
pounds, and they are brilliantly colored—horizon blue, blaze orange,
sunset red, and sometimes a combination of the first and last. They
don't seem natural to me, probably because I started hiking in the
years when they weren't necessary.

But if a hiker refuses to carry a tent, in these populous times, he
must arrive at his destination very early in the day. Otherwise he
won't find a place to lay his sleeping bag down. So I asked: "How
many people at Eliza Brook last night?"

"Six or seven," the lads assured me. "And the swimming is good."

In return I told them that they could reach the highway in fifteen or
twenty minutes (they were younger and they were going downhill)
and that the trail was excellent all the way. Then we parted, each
having heard the news that would cheer him the most.

The heat was oppressive along the trail, which was still bordered
with hardwoods for the most part, rising to spruce from time to time
but always descending to birch again. My thighs told me that I had
been humping the ridgeline long enough. At eleven-thirty by Sally's
watch (she'd loaned it to me in parting) I stopped for lunch at a
boulder which offered both a breeze and an overlook. I might have
been in Tennessee. The day was sultry, and the mountains too had
the look of Tennessee, lushly green in the foreground but shading
quickly to gray.

The overlook confirmed what my thighs had told me. The
customary trail map is based on hundred-foot contours, which is fine
for major changes in elevation but not very helpful on a bumpy
stretch. A trail that appears flat on the map can actually consist of
endless bumps of one hundred feet—which is to say: climb a ten-story
building and go down the other side—one after the other. This was
the case along the Kinsman Ridge. It was decidedly rougher than the
map had suggested.

I lunched on pemmican. There are many recipes for pemmican, and I had chosen one that called for a mixture of dried fruit, nuts, and freeze-dried bacon bar, all jumbled together and run through a meat grinder. From the first taste, I knew that the recipe was too rich in sunflower seeds. The smell of sunflower oil was overpowering, and the taste nearly so. That was too bad, because I would have no opportunity to improve it until I reached Crawford Notch in six days' time. Nor did I have any other food. As with mountain tents, so with mountain stoves: I had done most of my hiking in the campfire days. Rather than carry one of those marvels of Swedish engineering, the brass stoves that had replaced the campfire, I would eat dry food except when I crossed a highway or stopped at one of the hostels maintained by the Appalachian Mountain Club. Then I would gorge myself. I have always been skinny; I figured that the weight loss would not harm my appearance to any great degree. But I had not realized that my pemmican would be so unsavory.

It was also extremely dry. I flushed it down with water from my canteen, and completed the meal with two salt tablets. Then I left the overlook and the black flies which had located me as soon as I sat down. July is the black-fly season in the White Mountains.

For some time I had noticed queer footprints along the trail. Instead of the waffle-shaped impressions of the standard hiking boot— all of which are soled with a patented material called Vibram—these footprints were flat, with circular impressions the size of a nickel. They looked like the spoor of gym shoes, which proved to be exactly what they were. Dropping down into yet another depression which did not show on the map, I heard voices and caught the nostalgic smell of woodsmoke. Four young men were sitting in the trail, and *they had a campfire*. Campfires are definitely not the style in the White Mountains any more, again because the traffic is too heavy. A campfire at noon on a muggy day is even more to be wondered at. Furthermore, these hikers weren't cooking anything; they were just sitting around their fire in the middle of the trail, presumably under the impression that was what one did in the mountains.

"Keeping warm?" I asked. I thought this very funny, but they did not. They stared at me, more suspicious than hostile, as if fearing that I might ask to see their campfire permit. Or perhaps they hadn't expected to meet anyone on the trail, let alone a middle-aged man in a smiley-faced T-shirt. (I had chosen it for underwear because its basic color was gray.) I tried again: "Do you know how far it is to Gordon Pond Trail?" I had been looking forward to this side-trail for an hour, figuring that it marked the halfway point between the highway and Eliza Brook Shelter.

"We don't know what's ahead," they admitted. So I told them what I knew about the trail and the shelter, wished them a good day, and hiked up another rise.

In a few minutes I passed the side-trail to Gordon Pond—halfway home!—and some time later I found another lookout boulder. This one was on the flank of Mt. Wolf, the only named peak in the four miles I had traveled, and still not impressive enough to have its elevation shown on the map. I reckoned it to be 3,500 feet. From my boulder I could see Gordon Pond to the south, larger than I had expected; and I could hear the sound of an axe. *Chop . . . chop.* Were the four hikers gathering wood for their fire? Or was the mythical trail crew back at work, having emerged from its hiding place now that I had passed?

The trail went generally downhill from Mt. Wolf, but still with those tedious ups and downs—more ups than I cared to see. I was hot; I was thirsty; and I was very definitely weary in the legs. Nor was the footing as easy as it had been. The trail meandered east and west across the ridge, and it was tricky with roots and stones—more like a bushwhack route than the manicured path I'd followed until now. Had I gone astray? No, because from time to time I sighted Bog Pond through the trees, just where it should have been. I decided that a trail crew was indeed working its way along the ridge, and that I had leap-frogged it.

Each time I sighted Bog Pond, it seemed no closer than the time before. According to my map, a power line crossed the trail at this low spot on Kinsman Ridge, looping through the mountains from North Woodstock to the village of Easton. Normally I would have been outraged by the sight of high-tension wires above a mountain trail. Not today: they would be my final landmark on the way to Eliza Brook Shelter, and I was positively anxious to see them.

First, though, I met a young woman coming up the trail, dressed in street clothes and carrying a red ditty bag. "You're traveling light," I said. She told me that they were on a day hike of the ridge: she was being followed at some little distance by her husband or boyfriend, who was stripped to the waist, sweating mightily, and looking very much like a man in want of a cool beer. No doubt I looked the same, but I had one mile to go and he had six.

Then I walked down to the Bog Pond lowlands, to the marsh grass and the power lines—not the great metal cribs I had expected, either, but slender gray poles topped by chocolate-brown insulators. To be sure, the nearest set was hard by the Appalachian Trail, but it could have been worse. The "Bog Pond Corridor" was being considered as an alternate route for Interstate 93 on its journey from North Woodstock to Littleton, if the highwaymen were barred from Franconia Notch. In the silence of the marsh, broken only by a mosquito's whine, I envisioned an expressway through this place, and I didn't like it much. What would happen to the trail, for example? Surely the highwaymen wouldn't build a footbridge for the few hundred hikers who passed through here in a season. Would we be expected to dodge

the traffic on our way to Eliza Brook Shelter? Or would the lean-to
become a rest area on I-93, a sort of zoological garden where the
tourists could observe the backpackers in their native habitat?

No, there were better uses for "Bog Pond Corridor" than covering
it with asphalt. I was enjoying one of those uses, walking uphill
again and listening for the sound of Eliza Brook running clear. At
last I heard the stream, and at last I plodded up the side-trail to the
lean-to where I would spend the night.

It was three o'clock—five hours since Sally had dropped me at
Kinsman Notch. I was a bit humbled by my progress. The *AMC
White Mountain Guide,* the fat little book with orange covers from
which I was plotting my course, suggested that I should have covered
the distance in four hours. (The trail times are worked out according
to formula, two miles per hour over level ground, plus thirty minutes
for each thousand feet that must be climbed.) I had overshot my
allowance by 25 percent. It didn't matter today, since Eliza Brook
Shelter was empty, but there were some days ahead when I planned to
walk for six or seven hours, and on more popular trails than this one.
If I had to extend those days by 25 percent, I would have to rise very
early in the morning.

I unrolled my sleeping bag against one wall, to claim that relatively private space for myself. Then I took off my boots, socks, and
smiley-faced undershirt, hanging them on the bushes to dry. Then I
scrambled down the embankment to cool myself in Eliza Brook. I
filled my canteen, too, and regretfully added five Halazone tablets to
the water. In the good old days, circa 1965, I wouldn't have insulted
mountain water with chemicals, but much had changed since then.

The changes weren't obvious here, probably because the lower part
of Kinsman Ridge was not much hiked except by those who were fascinated by the Appalachian Trail. It wasn't truly wilderness, as witness the power lines. It wasn't very mountainous, either, as witness
the fact that no altitude was given for Mt. Wolf. In the Northeast, a
mountain is generally considered to be something taller than four
thousand feet, unless it is beautiful like Chocorua or isolated like
Grand Monadnock. Mt. Wolf was neither. It was merely a high spot
on the ridge.

*At Bog Brook,
an alternate
corridor for
the interstate,
high-tension
wires reach
across the
Appalachian
Trail*

The register showed that on most nights, as those southbound
hikers had promised, no more than six or seven persons slept at Eliza
Brook Shelter.

I mixed a cup of Tang. Though I can manage without hot food, or
indeed without any food except pemmican, I cannot do without
Tang in the mountains. It is the only way to make water palatable in
quantities large enough to quench my thirst. As it happened, I had
grossly overestimated the amount of pemmican I could eat, while
grossly underestimating my requirements for Tang. I drank two cups
in fifteen minutes. (Actually it wasn't the brand-name product but a

supermarket rival called Orange Flavored Breakfast Drink.) After the second cup, I realized that I must thin the brew henceforth, and consume no more than four or five cups a day. So I stowed the plastic bottle in my pack and explored Eliza Brook Shelter.

There are about sixty shelter sites in the White Mountains, half of them maintained by the U.S. Forest Service and half by private organizations such as the Appalachian Mountain Club. (The responsibility for maintaining the trails is similarly divided between public and private agencies.) In addition, the AMC operates eight high-country "huts" at which a hiker can purchase both food and lodging. These might more properly be called hostels. They are intended for travelers who wish to hike in comparative luxury.

A shelter offers no amenities beyond a roof, a fireplace, and a latrine. Generally it is designed as a lean-to, with a sleeping platform and an open front, but the variations are so numerous that it is rare to find two shelters exactly alike. The one at Eliza Brook was the traditional lean-to, with a roof of metal and sides of vertical logs. There was a plank floor for sleeping. Ten years ago, the planks would have been padded by successive layers of spruce and fir, and I would have added a fresh layer for myself. But bough beds, like campfires, have gone out of fashion. The wilderness can't afford them. An AMC official once estimated that if every hiker cut wood for a fire and boughs for a mattress, the pillage would resemble the timber rape of 1900—which was the reason for setting aside the White Mountain as a wilderness reserve.

So I would have no fragrant mattress of boughs. Instead I would unroll a foam pad, 48″ long, 20″ wide, and 1½″ thick, just enough to cushion my spine. If I had been younger, I would have slept on bare planks rather than carry such a luxury. But I was not younger—I was older, in fact. The forties are the decade in which a man learns to compromise.

In front of the lean-to was a stone fireplace, and the stones were actually mortared into place. There was even a grill—also mortared into place, as if the AMC feared that somebody might run off with it. (The fear would not be altogether unreasonable, considering the vandalism the AMC has experienced at its hostels and shelters.) There was some charred wood and a few bits of rubbish in the fireplace, but nothing like the mess that I expected to find at an unsupervised campsite. Each year there are fewer such campsites, especially along heavily traveled routes like the Appalachian Trail. Some shelters have been demolished; others have been improved with tent platforms and caretakers. I would not sleep at another unsupervised campsite until I reached Desolation Shelter in the Pemigewasset Wilderness, five days hence.

A dog came up the trail and looked me over. This was Bimbo, as it turned out, and he belonged to a young man in green work clothes who followed him to the lean-to. Bimbo's owner was part of the trail crew whose work I had seen and whose axes I had heard, the other side of Mt. Wolf. He said that they were a Forest Service crew, not part of the AMC, which explained the chainsaw wounds on the logs I had crossed. They were camped by Gordon Pond and were working their way northward along the ridge.

"Hey," he said when I complimented him on the stonework coming up from Kinsman Notch, "you should see what we did last year on Beaver Brook Trail." I said that I had missed it—that I meant to come over Mt. Moosilauke, but had skipped that section because I wasn't sure if Beaver Brook Shelter was still in business. "Oh, it's there all right," he said. "We're improving this whole section of trail, you know. The Forest Service got a special appropriation because the Appalachian Trail belongs to the government now." He meant that Congress had declared it to be a National Scenic Trail. Where it passes through the national forest, it is a restricted zone where no trailside camping, logging, or motorized traffic is allowed. Along with this protective umbrella, apparently, goes a budget to make the Appalachian Trail more comfortable for pedestrians.

"Did you see four hikers coming this way?" I asked. "One of them was wearing gym shoes."

"I saw them. They were starting to make camp, but I told them the shelter was just ahead."

Not long after Bimbo and his owner had left, the four young men straggled in. It was five o'clock by Sally's watch. They'd started yesterday from Kinsman Notch, tenting overnight on the trail and breaking camp at nine o'clock this morning, while I was still on the interstate. I felt much better about the time it had taken me to reach Eliza Brook Shelter.

They were from Hamden, Connecticut; they'd never been to the mountains before; and they were hiking with the aid of a road map that showed the Appalachian Trail as a pretty red line through the wilderness. "I'm a pilot," one of them said—a bushy-haired man with a homely and happy face, though far from happy at the moment. "I've flown over the mountains, you know, and I thought how *green* they were. But now that I'm walking through 'em, my feet hurt." No wonder. In addition to tents, they were carrying hatchets, sheath knives, two pounds of spaghetti, two large cans of tomato sauce, and three quarts of water for the pilot alone. In addition to flying small planes, he worked in a factory where the temperature was at fever heat, and he was in the habit of drinking a gallon of water each day. While he massaged his feet, his comrades pitched the tents and cut wood for a fire. The nearest deadwood was in the retaining wall which kept the lean-to from tumbling into Eliza Brook, so they took a log out of that and chopped it into fireplace lengths.

27

Two pounds of pasta is too much, even for four young men with heavy packs, so I dined heartily on the leftovers. What I couldn't eat, the Hamden Four threw into the fireplace. (Not a bad practice, actually. If you don't "carry out what you carry in," as the signs advise, you should at least burn the stuff, to keep bears and raccoons away from the campsite.) We were a bit hasty in cleaning up. Two more hikers came up the trail at seven o'clock—tired, dirty, and looking very hungry indeed.

"That's a long seven miles," I said to them.

"It sh-sh-sh-*sure* as hell is!" the leader exploded. He was so skinny as to make me look plump; his hair was long uncut, hanging in ringlets to his shoulders and only partly restrained by a dirty blue sweatband. He wore shorts, and his legs were ravaged by insect bites. His companion was smaller and quieter, and for a long time I honestly couldn't decide whether he was male or female. Male, as it turned out. The two of them had come all the way from Glencliff today, covering not only the seven miles between here and Kinsman Notch, but the seven miles over Mt. Moosilauke as well. What's more, they had taken time out to hitchhike into North Woodstock.

They were Through Hikers.

The through hiker   iii

Of all the characters you can meet in the mountains, the Through Hiker is at once the strangest
and most enviable.

"I left Georgia in February," said the older
man, whose name was Thom Connelly, when I
expressed surprise at seeing him so early in the
season. The typical Through Hiker starts the trek
in April, follows the sun northward, and reaches
the White Mountains after the black flies have
ceased to pillage the countryside. Wasn't there
snow on the ground in February? "Damned
right," Thom Connelly said. "The guy going

through in front of me was k-k-k-*killed* in a blizzard, and I had to take ten days out to help locate the body." He said this with considerable satisfaction, while digging through his pack for food. Like me, he was stoveless. He and his companion—Bobby Ramsey, his nephew, who had joined him in Massachusetts—were subsisting on a pemmican that was scarcely more handsome than mine, though it was not ground up. About once a week they hitchhiked into town and bought a new supply of peanuts, chocolate, and other dry foods, treating themselves meanwhile to a bowl of soup and two hotdogs apiece. That had been their mission in North Woodstock. So they'd covered in a day what I would have covered in two, and they'd gone shopping besides. I felt humble once more.

As for the Hamden Four, they were awestruck. They'd never seen anything so wild, dirty, or fabulous as Thom Connelly and young Bobby Ramsey. "Well, it's too bad you didn't get here earlier," one of them said. "We had a lot of spaghetti and we just threw it out."

Thom Connelly looked at him in disgust. "Muh-muh-*man*," he said. "Never throw anything out until you break camp in the morning." Having educated them in the etiquette of the Appalachian Trail, he then proceeded to discover what each of them did in life. "Where you from, man?" he asked. "What d'you do?" He skipped me, though. Whereas the young men from Hamden were pilots, short-order cooks, factory workers, and late blooming college students, I was clearly none of these things. Probably Thom Connelly didn't ask because he was afraid he'd be unable to conceal his scorn for the answer. Insurance salesman? Lawyer? Writer of a journal about a hundred-mile walk through the White Mountains?

I was just as happy to be left out of the biography session. It is a habit that journalists acquire, that of pretending they are invisible. Like a good journalist, though, I asked Thom Connelly what he did when he was not hiking the Appalachian Trail.

"Oh," he said, "I go to the University of Alaska—when I go."

The Hamden Four were more interested in his pack, since theirs weighed more than forty pounds apiece.

"Too much," Thom Connelly told them. "Max . . . thirty-five pounds max, and that's after I've bought food. Usually it's more like thirty pounds." No, he didn't carry a tent. When caught without shelter he slept under a GI poncho—army *surplus*, he said with emphasis, to affirm that he'd no closer attachment to the fascists at Fort Dix. Nor did he carry a canteen, only a cup. What happened when he walked all day without crossing a stream? "Impossible, man," he said. "Anyhow, I can go seven hours without water, but I don't like to." And yes, his feet were blistered, but only because his boots had begun to wear out in Pennsylvania and he had finally replaced them in the first large town he came to, which was Hanover, New Hampshire. They weren't a good fit, and Thom Connelly was gorgeously profane about the mountain wisdom of Hanover in general and the Dartmouth Outing Club in particular. "In two thousand miles," he said, "I only luh-luh-*lost* my way one time, and that was on the DOC trail from Hanover to Glencliff."

"Is anybody else walking the whole trail?" the pilot wanted to know.

Thom Connelly threw up his arms, which were not much thicker than broomsticks. "Hell, man," he said. "There must be twenty of them within sixty miles of here."

At eight o'clock we went to bed, the Hamden Four in their tents behind the lean-to, I against the right-hand wall, the Through Hiker and his nephew to the left. I said goodnight.

"Yeah," Thom Connelly agreed. "Have a good night, man."

Kinsman Ridge is the western wall of Franconia Notch, with Franconia Ridge providing the same service on the east. Is it a rule that all mountains run from north to south? Certainly they follow that policy in New Hampshire, perhaps because that is the way the glaciers moved, gouging the notches as they advanced and retreated. (Unlike the Rockies and the Alps, the White Mountains were not thrust out of the earth. Instead they were whittled down from the high lands which once dominated these parts.) The major peaks on the ridge ahead of me were South Kinsman, North Kinsman, and Cannon. Across the way were Flume, Liberty, Lincoln, and the great haystack of Mt. Lafayette.

I rolled out of Eliza Brook Shelter at seven o'clock, packed my sleeping gear, ate a handful of pemmican, and was ready to go. "See you at the next shelter, man." Thom Connelly said.

"If not before," I said, fully expecting that he would pass me before I was well warmed up. As for the Hamden Four, I doubted that I would ever see them again, so I left them with a schedule of trails and mileposts on the way to Franconia Notch, about nine miles from here. They were mightily impressed that I could delve this information from my little orange guidebook.

"Hey," the pilot marveled, "those maps show *everything*."

Not quite everything. They didn't show the bumps that made yesterday so wearisome, nor those that would weary us today.

The beginning was auspicious. The trail followed Eliza Brook upstream for about a mile, most pleasantly; I filled my canteen at the final crossing and began the ascent to South Kinsman. It was a hike such as I like best. Steep, but not so steep that I had to scramble; and steady, with every vertical foot a permanent gain, not to be lost by dropping down again. From an open spot below the summit, I saw Bog Pond and the power line, which looked like a brown road snaking along the low ground. There was no other sign of man, because the folds in the White Mountains are such that the roads are almost never visible. But while I was standing there, I was bothered by the whine of a helicopter, like a mosquito in my ear. It continued to pester me as I climbed, and sometimes I saw it through the trees: a little Bell with a bubble cockpit and a skeleton tail. It seemed to be scouting the ridgeline.

The summit of South Kinsman was open and flat, and there I met two day hikers from Lonesome Lake Hut. They told me that the guest list last night had amounted to six. I was glad to hear it, because I planned to sleep at the hut but had made no reservation. An AMC hut, like a Holiday Inn, likes to book its customers in advance.

I asked the day hikers about the helicopter. "Oh," they said, "it's probably hauling crapper barrels."

"I didn't see any barrel."

"Well, maybe it hasn't made the pick-up yet."

They didn't seem to find anything strange in the idea that a hundred-thousand-dollar helicopter should be sent into the mountains to pick up drums of human waste. Personally, I was convulsed. Here we were, three hikers questing for wilderness, and yonder was the technological marvel—more sophisticated than any suburban toilet—that kept the wilderness pure.

The black flies had staked a claim to South Kinsman. They were slow-moving and easy to squash, but they made up in numbers what they lacked in speed. Three hundred years ago, John Josselyn had remarked on this feature of July in the White Mountains. The black flies, he reported, "were so numerous . . . that a man cannot draw his breath, but he will suck of them in." So I moved on. The trail was both wider and deeper than it had been on the south slope—testimony to the number of hikers who had bagged the Kinsmans the easy way, from the north. As I descended into the col and climbed again, I wondered what was keeping Thom Connelly and Bobby Ramsey. They should have passed me long since.

The summit of North Kinsman is wooded, but with an outlook to the east, and that outlook is grand. For the first time I could see the whole sweep of Franconia Ridge, from Liberty to Mt. Lafayette. On this side of the notch, and far below me, was the gem of water that was Lonesome Lake, and northward was the deceptively gentle climb to Cannon Mountain. In all that vista, the only man-made thing was the observation tower on the round summit of Cannon. I decided to wait for Thom Connelly in this magnificent spot. But once again I was driven off: the air was full of insects, including that mosquito of a helicoptor, which was still barging about Kinsman Ridge.

The day, like yesterday, was hot. I swallowed water and salt tablets at regular intervals, especially after I moved off the summit and into the airless passage between the trees.

I met two hikers (one with a Captain America pack, all stars and stripes) who planned to spend the night on North Kinsman. They weren't especially happy to see me. As a solo hiker, and one who did most of his walking in the old days, I was delighted to meet somebody on the trail. It was like "speaking" a ship at sea. The event was so rare that good manners impelled us to heave to, to exchange the news and perhaps messages for home. The new breed of hiker did not seem to feel this way. At some point in the past ten years, *too many* faces had appeared on the trail, and they had become objects to be passed with scarcely a nod.

I had better luck at Kinsman Junction, where I met a police dog and its owner, a tourist in a golfing cap. He was enchanted to see a real hiker. He told me that he'd come up from the highway, that he'd passed Kinsman Pond Shelter, and that it had struck him as a very hot and buggy place. That confirmed my decision to sleep at Lonesome Lake Hut. When we parted, I thanked the golfer by telling him that if his ambition was to meet a real hiker, he should keep an eye out for Thom Connelly.

Kinsman Junction is a four-cornered intersection. I left the ridge on the Fishin' Jimmy Trail. According to the AMC Guide, Fishin' Jimmy was "the chief character in one of Annie Trumbull Slosson's stories," which left me no wiser than before. The trail proved to be tortuous, in bad repair, and with plenty of those tedious ups and downs. So it was a long while before I hiked up to a spruce grove and saw the roof of Lonesome Lake Hut. And such a roof! Lonesome has eight sides and a roof that is eight-pitched in consequence, with a skylight where the segments meet. It is a lovely building, if not exactly in the White Mountains tradition.

My first business at the hostel was to draw a glass of pink lemonade—free to overnight guests, as a hand-lettered sign informed me. I drank the first glass standing there. It was warm, of course, but the passion for iced drinks (like the sound of automobiles) is something that can be left behind in fifteen minutes of hiking.

I carried the second glass outside to enjoy with a cigarette. Most hikers do not smoke, and some are evangelical in their hatred of the weed, so I am very secretive about my habit when I am in the mountains. I do not smoke in the huts and shelters unless a smoker's corner has clearly been established by somebody else, and accepted by the others. At Lonesome, I sat on the outside steps. And there I sighted the Through Hiker, staggering down through the trees. Until now I was convinced that Thom Connelly and Bobby Ramsey had passed me somewhere, perhaps while I was at the overlook on North Kinsman. But here they were. "Muh-muh-*man!*" exploded Connelly when he threw down his pack. "That's a rough trail."

Is it astonishing that I had outwalked the Through Hiker? I thought so for ten minutes. Then the Hamden Four limped down to join us. Apparently they had learned something about mountain travel today—that it was natural to suffer a little. When they had a

Through Hiker in front of them, the Hamden Four could hump the ridge as fast as anyone.

"You spending the night here?" Connelly asked me.

"Yes."

"How much do they charge?"

"About twelve dollars for a bunk and two meals."

"Jesus," he said, "What a rip-off!" He sat down on the steps beside me and opened a can of pears. I recognized that can: the bushy-haired pilot had carried it as far as Eliza Brook Shelter but was unwilling to carry it any farther. He'd put it on the shelf, and of course Connelly had picked it up. He ate the pears now. I don't remember what we talked about in that interval, ranged on the steps of Lonesome Lake Hut like the spectators at a football game, except that it was the conversation of friends. Our only bond was Eliza Brook Shelter, but in the mountains that is bond enough.

Thom Connelly and Bobby Ramsey had abandoned their plan of pushing through to Mt. Liberty today. They too had learned something about the White Mountains of New Hampshire—that the miles are longer here. The Through Hikers would walk down to Lafayette Campground, to sleep beneath their ponchos in the company of Airstream trailers and Winnebago motor homes. The Hamden Four went with them.

"Goodbye," I said. "Have a good trip."

"Yeah, man," Thom Connelly said. "See you at the next shelter."

I didn't, though. I never saw him again, and I can only assume that he reached Mt. Katahdin on schedule, on the fourth of August, twenty-seven days out from Eliza Brook Shelter and six months after he'd left Springer Mountain in Georgia.

Hut persons

Franconia Notch is blessed with three lakes—
Echo, Profile, and Lonesome. The first two
belong to the car-borne tourist, while the third
reserves its beauty for those ambitious enough to
hike more than a mile from the highway and a
thousand feet up. For that reason alone, I
prefer it to the others.

Lonesome Lake is a tarn, which is a good
Yankee word for a mountain pond, and one that
somehow suggests the blackness of such ponds.
(They look like saucers of strong tea. Which in
fact they are, with decaying moss for the tea bag.)

As the footpath goes, Lonesome Lake is three-quarters of a mile around, with Cannon Mountain rising steeply to the north and the Franconia Ridge gorgeous to the east. Like a misplaced pagoda, the AMC hut commands the southern shore. A beaver appears regularly at dinner time and slaps his tail for the guests.

The lake, like the rest of Franconia Notch, is owned by the New Hampshire Division of Parks.* So it offers some amenities that are most unusual in the mountains. They include two aluminum rowboats and a raft for swimmers. . . . Swimming! Virtually every spring, brook, and pond in the White Mountains goes sooner or later to feed somebody's kitchen, with the result that a thoughtful hiker seldom bathes while he is on the trail. So it was with something approaching ecstasy that I waded into Lonesome Lake that Tuesday afternoon. The mud oozed deliciously between my toes. I walked out to Jockey-short depth, then rolled like a seal in the dark water, not so much swimming in the stuff but purely and simply dunking myself in it.

There was nobody on the trail when I emerged. I shucked my underwear and put on my jeans, marveling at how simple life could be, and I strolled up to the hostel to register for the night.

"Do you have a reservation?" the hutboy asked. He was a shaggy-haired young man with a green T-shirt and the regulation apron. The T-shirt said AMC CROO in white letters.

"No."

"Oh," he said. "A walk-in."

"Is that bad?"

"Well, it makes it hard to plan dinner."

"I'm mostly interested in a place to sleep," I said. "I'll skip dinner if that's any help."

The big landowner in the White Mountains, of course, is the U.S. Forest Service, which holds title to 730,000 acres. The New Hampshire Division of Parks controls all of Franconia Notch, half of Crawford Notch, and the summit of Mt. Washington. Other large tracts are owned by such public-spirited organizations as the Appalachian Mountain Club, Dartmouth College, and the Society for the Protection of New Hampshire Forests. The hiker seldom knows or cares where the boundaries are, and the owners themselves aren't always certain. (There is a $20 fine for unauthorized camping in a state park. When this penalty was first levied, the boundaries assumed a fresh importance, and only then did anyone realize that it was unclear where Franconia Notch State Park left off and the national forest began.) As far as the hiker is concerned, the White Mountains constitute a wilderess reserve of about 800,000 acres. That works out to 1,250 square miles, or more land that can be found in the state of Rhode Island.

"No, we'll manage," he said. He gave me a form to fill out and assigned me to bunkroom two, which I would share with two young men who were hiking the chain of huts from here to Carter Notch.

The AMC has eight of these mountain hostels, plus its base lodge at Pinkham Notch Camp. Taken together, they are like beads upon the necklace that is the Appalachian Trail, strung through the major ridges of the White Mountain National Forest. Thus it is possible to make the grand traverse without carrying anything heavier than a toothbrush and a checkbook. And the checkbook isn't entirely necessary. The AMC has a billing service, if it comes to that.

The Appalachian Mountain Club was established a century ago, though not for the purpose of engaging in the hostel business. That came about by accident. Frederick W. Kilbourne told the story in his *Chronicles of the White Mountains,* published in 1916:

"The project of forming an organization 'for the advancement of the interests of those who visit the mountains of New England and adjacent regions, whether for the purpose of scientific research or for summer recreation,' had been for some time a subject of discussion among scientists and others residing in or near Boston who were mountain-lovers. . . . The initiative came from Professor E.C. Pickering, who, on January 1, 1876, issued fifty cards of invitation to a meeting, at the Massachusetts Institute of Technology." Pickering was elected president, of course, and the AMC had a natural bias toward the scientific side of things. But scientists are like the rest of us: they don't enjoy being cold and wet in the mountains. The AMC soon decided to build "a stone hut or cabin" near Mt. Madison in the Northern Presidentials.

"The advisability and feasibility of having a place of refuge at this point having been demonstrated, construction was begun in August, 1888, the masons going into camp on the 21st and finishing the walls in about three weeks." Madison Hut proved so popular that it was enlarged by the construction of a women's bunkroom. Then a second hut was built near the first, this one containing the caretaker's quarters, a kitchen, and a dining room.

So the refuge had become a hostel in less than a generation. The AMC undertook its new mission with zeal. When Carter Notch Hut was built in 1914, it provided accommodations for thirty-six hikers. Then came a hut at Lakes of the Clouds, on the southern flank of Mt. Washington. When the first guests arrived in August of 1915, they found that it was equipped with "somewhat higher stone walls . . . and, as a special constructive feature, with several large plate-glass windows. . . . In the lighter and otherwise more attractive interior thus made possible, a person imprisoned during a driving tempest would have a rather pleasant experience, being able not only to stay there in comparative comfort, but also to watch the antics of the storm."

At the same time, the AMC installed a radio in each of the huts. Hikers could thus reserve their bunks in advance. "It is one of the ambitions of this benevolent organization," Kilbourne concluded, "to establish a chain of huts and camps throughout the Mountains as one of its agencies for . . . cultivating the tramping habit and the love of woods and mountains."

That ambition has been triumphantly achieved. The hut system is a considerable business these days, and AMC newsletters sometimes take on the flavor of a report to the stockholders: "1971 was another record year, with more than 30,000 hikers spending a night in a hut and another 75,000 climbers stopping by during the day. Pinkham alone had more than 100,000 people pass through its facilities last year. Our budget, a quarter of a million dollars, reflects the above use and shows the amount of money involved in our operation." That was 1971. Within three years the gross had doubled, and it will probably hit the million-dollar mark before long. Most of the hostels are now open in the spring and fall, though usually without meal service; two of them are open all winter. And the facilities at Pinkham Notch Camp have been greatly expanded.

Lonesome Lake Hut is the southwestern anchor of this enterprise. The hostel is an easy walk from US 3, over graded footpaths, so it might be expected to be the busiest in the chain. It isn't. Because it is so close to the highway, there's no reason to stay there unless you are coming up from the south, as I was, or unless you are introducing young children to the pleasures of hiking. The AMC therefore operates Lonesome as a "family camp"—for which it is perfectly designed, having the lake at its doorstep, being easy to reach, and being equipped with small bunkrooms instead of the usual dormitories. But there were no children today. The guests included my two roommates, two other backpackers, and a delegation of five AMC members from Connecticut. Business was so slack, in fact, that one bunkhouse had been turned over to a Forest Service crew that was working on this section of the Appalachian Trail.

Then there was me—the walk-in. I was mystified by my reception. It was not yet three o'clock in the afternoon; I was the tenth guest in a hostel designed for forty-six; and the dinner service at Lonesome was a one-pot casserole. Surely I was causing no inconvenience that could not be mended by throwing an extra handful of rice into the pot. Admittedly, the hutboy would have to accomplish this task unaided: his companions were absent on the annual hutboys' picnic. Perhaps that was the reason for his gloom.

I must stop saying *hutboy*. He was older than that, and furthermore two of his colleagues were women, as I discovered when they returned from the picnic. One of them ran the place. This was Liz Shultis, a pert young woman with black hair, who was more cordial to the walk-in. She offered to radio ahead to Greenleaf Hut to inform them I was coming for dinner on Wednesday. The hut-master there, she said, was Mike Schnitzer.

I'd met Mike the previous fall, when I was writing an article about the hut system. "Tell him it's the guy who spelled his name wrong," I told Liz. After some crosstalk on the radio (not all the huts can talk to each other, but must relay messages according to a crazyquilt but effective pattern) Liz reported that Mike was on his "days off," and that Greenleaf Hut was overbooked for Wednesday night. I would be sorry not to see Mike. I wanted to apologize for twisting his name in print, and I also wanted to say hello. He was a Harvard man and a good one, representing the new breed of AMC hutboy, the kind who took his job seriously and didn't look upon the guest as a natural enemy who was in the mountains for the sole purpose of inconveniencing AMC hutboys.

"Well," Liz Shultis suggested, "why don't you go up anyway? We'll probably have a storm, and maybe somebody won't show up."

That was what I wanted to hear.

There was a time when the AMC staffed its hostels almost exclusively with the preppies of New England, or at the very least with high-school boys who were bound for Dartmouth or another Ivy League college. Dartmouth and the AMC had a relationship that was very nearly incestuous. You were a hutboy before you went to Dartmouth; you were a skier and hiker while there; and afterward you went onto State Street in Boston—banker or lawyer or stockbroker—and you joined the AMC and sired youngsters who would become hutboys in turn, and so on through the generations. All that has changed. Both Dartmouth and the AMC hut system have gone co-educational in recent years. The crews are older, too, consisting of college students, dropouts, or recent graduates. (Dropouts are harder to find these days, by the way. That makes it hard to staff the huts in the off season.) Most of them are trained in the natural sciences, for the AMC expects its crews to be educators as well as pot-wallopers. And the atmosphere is not entirely Ivy League, either, though as a practical matter most of the crew members come from the eastern colleges. They are the ones who can show up for an interview.

For each opening in the hut system, there are twenty applications. It is not money but romance that attracts them. A rookie crew member earns about thirty dollars a week, plus room and board. They work eleven days on, three days off, and generally spend their free time hiking to the other huts . . . where they help with the chores.

These young people are the pack-mules of the White Mountains. Every egg consumed by the guests, every head of lettuce, every paper towel must be carried up the trail; and the hard trash must be carried down again. The packboard alone weighs twelve pounds and is handcrafted at Pinkham Notch Camp at a cost of sixty dollars in

43

labor and materials. Twice a week, on the average, the board and its owner are loaded with at least seventy-five pounds of perishables. Sometimes the load is ninety-five or a hundred pounds, and it makes no difference if the packer is female. She is expected to carry the up-bound freight, and she does.

"Carrying eggs is the most paranoid trip," one of the hutboys told me. "Thirty dozen at a time. Can you imagine what would happen if you fell?"

We filled only one table at dinner, with the food coming in great bowls from the head of the table. The main course was turkey casserole. It was preceded by fresh greens and followed by slabs of cake, with homemade bread on the side. I wolfed this food like a refugee. I could have gone through the meal a second time, with pleasure, except that I was too conscious of my status as a walk-in.

Over coffee I talked trails with the people from Connecticut. They were throwbacks to the 1950s, say, though only one of them was old enough to have been hiking then. This was the trail boss, Jean MacKesson. She said that the AMC Connecticut Chapter had sent a delegation to the White Mountains every summer for twenty years, to work on the trails, and that she had been on these trips every summer except one. The Connecticut people had even designed and constructed their own specialized tools for clearing brush.

Such people were once the backbone of the AMC, and at its Boston headquarters they still are. In the mountains, though, the professionals have taken over. The serious trail work is now done by hired help, whether in the employ of the AMC or that of the U.S. Forest Service, and the Forest Service crews are equipped with chainsaws and even portable jackhammers. Hiking has gone the way of downhill skiing. One group of people builds the trails and an entirely different group travels over them, so that—with the exception of Jean MacKesson and a few others—we have quite lost touch with the grubby work that makes our pleasure possible.

After dinner I read old copies of the AMC magazine, *Appalachia*. I was trying to fathom a bushwhack route to the Old Man of the Mountains. There is no trail to the Old Man, probably because the Cannon Cliffs are too steep for amateurs to meddle with; but I had always wanted to pay my respects to the profile that is New Hampshire's trademark, and I meant to try it in the morning.

The Lonesome crew and the Connecticut volunteers became interested in the project. Somebody turned up a copy of *Appalachia* that described a dozen rock-climbing routes on the Cannon Cliffs, including one that terminated on the Old Man's forehead. There was no mention of an approach from above. Still, if rock-climbers made a habit of scaling the cliffs, they must have been able to go the extra half-mile to the east summit, from which I would be approaching the profile.

Somebody else produced a U.S. Geological Survey map of the Franconia area, with forty-foot contour lines, and therefore more informative than the usual trail maps. And one of the crew (he who had signed me in) said that he'd once set out to find the Old Man, and that there was only one side-trail in the neighborhood of East Cannon. This was the same path, we decided, that was mentioned in the AMC Guide: "an obscure side-trail, marked with occasional cairns, continues straight ahead out upon the ledges to the SE." I decided to start with that. The Old Man was to the north, but it might be easier to follow the open ledge than to bushwhack through trees and scrub.

With my compass and the survey map, I memorized the geography of the Cannon Cliffs. When the summit of Mt. Lafayette was due east, I would be in a direct line with the Old Man. Then all I had to do was scramble down and stand on his forehead—being careful not to overstep the mark, for that would put me uncomfortably close to Profile Lake, one thousand feet below.

Finding the old man   v

It was in 1805 that the Old Man of the Mountains was first seen by an Anglo-Saxon. As the story goes, two road-builders went down to the shore of Echo Lake, looked up, and saw the great profile etched in stone. New Hampshire was never the same again. Some billions of souvenir ashtrays, liquor bottles, highway markers, insurance-company letterheads, and prose-poems have been based on that discovery. Franconia Notch State Park is based on it, and so is Interstate 93.

South of the notch, the village of Woodstock was settled about 1773. To the north, the village of Franconia was settled in 1774. The distance between those settlements is twenty miles, yet apparently no white man traveled that distance until 1800 or later. It is hard to believe that such a gorgeous and useful passage through the mountains could have been overlooked for an entire generation. Yet it seems to have happened that way. I have read Timothy Dwight's journals of two trips to the White Mountains, in 1797 and 1803, and in neither of them does he mention Franconia Notch or the Old Man of the Mountains. And Dr. Dwight was not a man to overlook the obvious.

The Indians must have known about the notch. We have the journal of the "ranging company" led by Captain Samuel Willard in 1725, one month from the Massachusetts settlements to the upper Pemigewasset. On Wednesday, September 29, the clerk made this entry in the journal: "We marched up the River about 14 mile, and come this day to the foot of a great mountain on the west side of the River, where the stream was small. We tracked Indians all this day which we suppose were gone directly to Canada; the mountains being steep and rocky, we could not track them further." Next morning the rangers "sent a scout of 20 men about 4 or 5 mile up the River who made no farther discovery." So they "left the River and steared East . . . and camped by reason of Rain." Had the rangers persisted, they would have reached the source of the Pemigewasset at Profile Lake, and they would almost certainly have pushed on through the notch—which, to an even greater certainty, was what the Indians had done.

We also have an Indian legend about the notch. However, like most such legends, it did not find its way into print until long after the Indians had been driven from the mountains. But it is a pretty story and worth telling on that account:

Pemigewasset—for whom a tribe and eventually the river were named—was an Abenaki chief who lived somewhere north of Franconia. He led his people in a long war against the Algonquin of New York State. He was lamed in one of these battles, and in the manner of chieftains everywhere he decided to stop the bloodshed by marrying the daughter of an Algonquin chief. This he did, winning not only peace but a bride whom he came to love more than life itself.

Years later, a messenger arrived to say that the Algonquin chief was dying and wished to see his daughter for the last time. Pemigewasset let her go, after receiving her pledge that she would meet him in the notch at the harvest moon. Pemigewasset was waiting at the appointed time, but his wife did not appear. Finally he sent his warriors home. He climbed to the highest ledge, vowing to wait there until he saw the signal fires of his wife's escort. Winter came and passed. In the spring, Pemigewasset's warriors climbed to the cliff and found the bones of their chief. These they reverently gathered and carried down to the lakeside for burial—whereupon they looked back and saw Pemigewasset's profile carved in stone, in everlasting vigil for his bride.

Wednesday morning early, I set out on the Hi-Cannon Trail. There were some glorious views from the ledges halfway up—Lonesome Lake below me and the Franconia Ridge beyond—but I didn't stop to admire them. I was anxious to find the Old Man before the weather broke, as it seemed likely to do. My pack was lean: poncho, map, compass, pemmican, and water. The rest of my gear I had left at the hut.

Thus lightened, I reached the summit just after nine. Cannon Mountain is served by an aerial tramway, called Murphy's Folly when it was built in the 1930s. Twin cable cars lift skiers to the summit in the winter months, tourists in the summer; Governor Francis Murphy got the idea on a trip to Switzerland, and he rammed the project through the state legislature against much opposition. The tramway has proved to be a splendid investment. It goes a long way toward subsidizing the entire state park system, and it has made Cannon second only to Mt. Washington as the New Hampshire peak most walked upon by man.

The tourists are more or less restricted to the Rim Trail, a gravel path supplied with benches and picnic tables. The main hiking trail joins this path for a short distance, then takes off eastward across the knoll that is East Cannon. The point of departure is unmarked, probably to discourage the tourists from straying in that direction. From this vantage I could see Greenleaf Hut where I hoped to be sleeping tonight. It stood just at treeline on Mt. Lafayette. As seen from the slopes of Cannon Mountain, Lafayette is the most handsome piece of real estate in New Hampshire. It was once called Great Haystack, and it is a pity the name was changed. It evokes so well the settlers of 1774, looking up at those massive shoulders and comparing them to the only thing in their experience that was at all similar—a great haystack.

I oriented myself and my map, decided that the Old Man was just beyond the east summit, and with that assurance I started down the hiking trail. It was not very easy to follow. I wondered what the "obscure side-trail" from East Cannon would be like.

It was good . . . for the first ten yards. Apparently everyone who hiked up from Profile Clearing stopped here for a time, to rest and to admire the view. Beyond the first outlook, though, the trail matched its description in the AMC Guide, except that there were no cairns. Following instinct more than anything else, I went down over ledges, through scrub and wild sedge, with just the faintest trace of a goatpath to show that other feet had passed this way, until I was looking down into the chasm that was Franconia Notch. The drop was sheer for six hundred feet. Then there was a talus slope of fallen rocks; then a brief margin of forest; then the highway, along which trucks were groaning audibly toward the height-of-land at Profile Clearing.

Franconia Notch is about six miles from south to north, climbing with the Pemigewasset to its source in Profile Lake. The Pemi flows eventually into the Merrimack River. A few thousand feet northward, Echo Lake feeds Lafayette Brook, which follows a different course to the Connecticut River. So the snowmelt and runoff from Franconia Notch provide drink, irrigation, power, transport, recreation, and occasional beauty to more than half the population of New England. . . . The sweat from my brow would reach the ocean at Newburyport, Mass. When I reached the Old Man, it would travel to the sea at Old Saybrook, Conn.

I turned north—and found a trail! There were also some eye-bolts sunk into the ledges. They served no discernible purpose, since by my reckoning the Old Man was still some distance beyond. I followed the trail northward, losing it and picking it up again (or picking up a different trail, for it was likely that more than one path had been worn along the rim). Only once did I have to bushwhack, and even there I was sure that somebody had passed that way before me. There seemed to be logic of a sort in the route I was following through the scrub.

Then, directly below me, I saw a man in a red shirt. He was prone on a ledge with his head and shoulders over the brink, and he seemed to be talking to someone below. I took him to be part of a rock-climbing team. I scrambled down to join him—which proved to be the hardest part of the trip so far, for the boulders here were a positive devil's den. Except for the lure of another human being, I wouldn't have attempted it, but would have continued to follow the rim northward.

When I finally gained the ledge, I found it very crowded. It was a shelf of granite about ten feet wide and twenty feet long, drooping both outward and northward. Down the center ran a plastic bandage. This was bridged with steel rods about three inches in diameter, fastened into the granite on either side, and equipped with great turnbuckles with which to tighten them. Workmen were walking over and around this steelwork, nine men altogether, with tools and lunchboxes and a packbasket or two. I had found the Old Man of the Mountains. What was more, I had arrived on the one day of the year when a crew from the highway department and state park system was checking the state of his health.

There is, of course, no profile on the Cannon Cliffs. "The marvel of this countenance," wrote the prose-poet of the White Mountains, Starr King, "is greatly increased by the fact that it is composed of three masses of rock which are not in perpendicular line with each other. On the brow of the mountain itself, standing on the visor of the helmet that covers the face, or directly underneath it on the shore of the little lake, there is no intimation of any human features in the lawless rock. Remove but a few rods either way from the guide-board on the road, where you are advised to look up, and the charm is dissolved."

Starr King was very particular about when the profile should be viewed: at four o'clock in the afternoon, and in the summer.

"The expression is really noble, with a suggestion partly of fatigue and melancholy. He seems to be waiting for some visitor or message. On the front of the cliff there is a pretty plain picture of a man with a pack on his back, who seems to be endeavoring to go up the valley. Perhaps it is the arrival of this arrested messenger that the old stone visage has been expecting for ages."

I for one have never seen that messenger, and there are some for whom the Old Man's expression is not noble, melancholy, or even fatigued. Fredrika Bremer, a Swedish novelist who toured the White Mountains in 1851, had this to say about the profile: "It has not any nobility in its features, but resembles a very old man in a bad humor and with a nightcap on his head, who is looking out from the mountain half inquisitive."

But perhaps Ms. Bremer was standing in the wrong place. If you move a short distance down the road, warned one of the Old Man's earliest admirers, the profile reverts to "a toothless old woman in a mob cap."

When I was in school, I worked one summer for the New Hampshire Division of Parks. The director then was Russell Tobey, who smoked bad cigars but who otherwise reminded me of a British ambassador, so silver-haired and distinguished was he. Mr. Tobey took a fond interest in the Old Man. One of his dreams was to charter a helicopter to photograph the profile from above. If the Old Man could be seen from one direction, Mr. Tobey reasoned, surely he could be seen from the other, perhaps when snow was one the ground. But he never found room in his budget for the experiment. The state parks were expected to pay their own way, and did, at least in those years.

I asked the workmen if they knew of anyone photographing the Old Man from the air. They looked at each other—those who weren't suspended from ropes or otherwise engaged. A spokesman was somehow chosen. "No," he said, a big man with a very large monkey wrench. "I never heard of *that*." He seemed sorry to disappoint me, and he added that I could see the Old Man's nose if I liked. All I had to do was lean over the ledge and look down to my left.

"I guess not," I said.

"No, maybe you shouldn't," he agreed.

As for the third ledge, the one that formed the Old Man's jaw, he had no idea where that was located. Neither did anyone else. They were specialists—brain surgeons, you might say—and their only concern was the fracture in the Old Man's pate.

By the 1920s, this crack was serious enough to be mended with chains. It kept deepening, however, as water ran into the opening and froze there in successive winters. No chain in the world is strong enough to withstand the power of frost. So Russell Tobey went to the state legislature in 1957, asking for $25,000 to be used in weather-proofing the Old Man. It isn't easy to obtain money from the New Hampshire legislature, but the profile is a special case. Daniel Webster once wrote of it: "Men hang out their signs indicative of their respective trades: shoemakers hang out a gigantic shoe; jewelers, a monster watch; and the dentist hangs out a gold tooth, but up in the mountains of New Hampshire, God Almighty has hung out a sign to show that there He makes men." As our ultimate billboard, the Old Man of the Mountains was well worth the expenditure of $25,000.

The work was done in the summer of 1958. Helicopters flew twenty tons of supplies to a sandbagged landing 500 feet above the Old Man. Fast-drying cement was used to plug the main fracture. Then it was capped with plastic and bridged with the steelwork I have described, and a concrete gutter was installed to divert the runoff from above. Finally, nineteen miscellaneous boulders were fastened with steel cables—a courtesy to rock-climbers, I suspect, since the boulders do not contribute to the profile.

Each summer, a crew visits the Old Man to tighten his tie-rods and to repair any weak spots in his bandage. The turnbuckles may be loosened by vibration from the highway below, or from natural causes. As for the bandage, it is not the elements or even the traffic that causes the damage, but man's urge to leave his name wherever he goes. Rock-climbers emerge upon this shelf; they are exultant; they take out their Swiss Army knives and carve names and dates in the most workable material at hand. In the case of the Old Man, the tablet is always the bandage that keeps him watertight.

"You'd think they'd have more sense," grumbled the man with the monkey wrench. "Look, there's a group from the Phillips Academy in Exeter—*they* should have more sense. And that one over there," he said, pointing to block letters a quarter-inch deep in the plastic. "I'm going to take a picture of that one. And if I ever catch up with him, he'll wish he was someplace else."

The workmen had brought along a gallon of epoxy resin, which they used to paint over the graffiti. I didn't stay long enough to see how they disposed of the container. I have been told that the original crew took the easy course and heaved their buckets down the cliff, so that the rocks below are smeared with plastic that will last a thousand years. This is hearsay evidence. I didn't have the time, equipment, or courage to investigate for myself.

Girl scouts and other cookies

Say what you will about Franconia Notch, it isn't wilderness. After retrieving my gear at the hostel, I followed Lonesome Lake Trail down to Lafayette Campground, emerging between site 93 and site 95. Families were lunching at picnic tables. The campground was an aluminum forest of motor homes, trailers, and pickup-truck rigs with decals of leaping deer upon the doors.

There was a telephone booth beside US 3. I'd promised to call Sally Wednesday afternoon to let her know I was on schedule, so I dropped my pack and walking stick outside the booth.

Feeling very strange about it, I searched for a dime in my pocket. It was the first coin I'd handled in three days, and it didn't work. Neither did the dime I borrowed from a passing tourist. Nothing worked with that telephone: *it was out of order.* Of course it was out of order! Wasn't that why we require these occasional flights to the mountains?

I walked back to the campground office, where a park ranger in khakis put me through to the tramway station, which in turn gave me an outside line. Afterward the ranger bawled me out for talking so long. "You weren't supposed to use that telephone anyhow," he reminded me.

> A telephone booth beneath the bough,
> A gift shop and thou,
> My love, beside me at the picnic table—
> Ah picnic table!—
> Were paradise enow.

As far as I am concerned, the highwaymen can have Franconia Notch. Its busiest moments, according to the experts who study such things, come on the Saturday before Columbus Day—the consequence of autumn foliage and a long weekend. On October 12, 1974, about sixteen thousand automobiles drove through the notch. If each contained one father, one mother, and one child (which seems a reasonable assumption) then the population of the state park that day was 48,000, making it one of the larger cities in New Hampshire. Suppose that half of them could have been diverted elsewhere by a circumferential highway. Franconia Notch would still have been a circus, and there would have been another circus in the Bog Pond Corridor or whatever alternate route had been chosen for I-93.

No. Keep the traffic in the notch. The Old Man of the Mountains hasn't had a quiet moment in a hundred years; he must be used to the excitement by now.

The Old Bridle Path begins just across the highway from Lafayette Campground. "No beast that was ever bridled," complained Albert Bushnell Hart in *The Nation* in 1896, "could make his way up that steep, stony, rough watercourse, choked with fallen trees." Near the highway it is now a graded path. Soon enough, however, I was walking in a bedrock trench, worn by the horses that once had carried tourists to the summit of Mt. Lafayette. Meanwhile the sky had changed from a milky blue to a creamy white. A sprinkle of rain began to fall. I climbed steadily, hoping to reach Greenleaf Hut before the promised thunderstorm.

There was one magnificent outlook. Unlike the views from Kinsman Ridge, this one showed the highway clearly, a shining ribbon along which toy automobiles and trucks were moving, down

to the Flume and North Woodstock, up to Lafayette Campground
and the tramway station. Across the way I could see Lonesome Lake
tucked between folds in the mountain, much as I had seen it yesterday
from North Kinsman. But from here the ridgeline of Cannon looked
to be the serious business that it was, bumping along on a steady
ascent to the lookout tower. Beyond the tower I could see the tramway summit station, and the steelwork and cables that supported the
cars. Below that was the great brown scar of the Cannon Cliffs. There
was no suggestion from here that the cliffs could have formed anything so remarkable as the Old Man of the Mountains.

I heard thunder, so I decided to move along. In hutboy parlance,
thunderstorms are known as "thumpers," just as the crew is known
as "da croo" and an unprepared hiker is known as a "goofer." Greenleaf Hut is a magnet for goofers. It is located at treeline on New
Hampshire's second mountain, but is much easier to reach than the
hostel on Mt. Washington. So on any fine day in Franconia Notch
(and on many not so fine) the sweatshirt-and-sneaker brigade goes up
for a look at a real AMC hut, and perhaps to stand on a mile-high
summit.

I met my first goofer just after leaving the overlook. He was upward bound, a heavyset young man in slacks and a short-sleeved
shirt; he was carrying a nylon windbreaker and a thermos bottle, and
he was in a hurry. "I want to get over the ridge before the lightning
hits," he told me. Then he added: "My mother is back there a ways.
She's fifty-three." Well, she had but ten years on me, but since he
clearly regarded fifty-three as an advanced age, I suggested that
maybe he shouldn't have left her on the trail. "Oh, she's doing just
fine," he said. "She climbed Mt. Washington last week."

Not long after this, the first lightning bolt hit the ridge, ahead of
me and to the left. The thunderclap rolled in without a pause, which
meant that the strike was close. Still, the trees were tall enough here
that the lightning, should it move this way, would probably choose
them instead of me as its conduit to the ground. Anyhow, like most
people I have an invincible faith that I won't be struck by lightning.
The young goofer was more cautious: hard on the heels of the
thunderclap, he reappeared on the trail like the Mad Hatter in search
of his tea party. "I think I'd better go back down," he said. Whereupon he dropped his thermos on the trail. There is no sadder sound
in all the world than the glass sloshing around in a thermos bottle. I'd
heard it many times in my schooldays, before I was man enough to
carry my milk in a whiskey bottle.

I trust that the goofer and his mother got back to the highway all
right. As for myself, I emerged with pleasing suddeness at treeline on
Mt. Lafayette, and there was the Greenleaf water tower, and there
were my two roommates from Lonesome Lake Hut, watching the
storm with their hair blowing in the wind and their hands in their

pockets. They said they'd come from Lonesome in two and a half hours. That was fast hiking, even for young lads with light packs.

Greenleaf is typical of the older, smaller hostels in the AMC chain. It was built in 1929, sleeps forty-five guests, and has a summertime crew of four. Its shingles have weathered to the gray-green of the surrounding rocks. From outside it doesn't seem large enough for such amenities, but it provides a kitchen, a common room, and sex-segregated bunkrooms and toilets. And it was overbooked. Nevertheless, my appearance caused much less dismay than it had at Lonesome Lake Hut. There is a saying that if you want to get a job done quickly, you should assign it to a busy man. By the same logic, if you want to stay at a hostel without a reservation, perhaps it is wise to pick the busiest hostel on the trail. Today that honor belonged to Greenleaf. An absent-minded clerk at Pinkham Notch Camp had accepted reservations from a group of ten, another group of twenty-three, the two lads from Lonesome, and an assortment of fourteen hikers who were coming from Galehead Hut, farther along the ridge. If they all showed up, I would be the fiftieth at dinner. This possibility didn't seem to bother the crew in the slightest.

Then there were the Girl Scouts from Illinois. The first of them wandered in just after rain began to lash the hut. They kept coming, fifteen of them in the next half hour; and last of all came the two matrons who were supposed to be leading them. My God. If the Hamden Four were unprepared for the mountains, what were the Girl Scouts from Illinois? They had no map of any kind. They'd set out to hike from Franconia Notch to Mt. Washington in *three days*, and they had begun this ambitious trek by spending four hours reaching treeline on their first mountain. For warmth they had such garments as quilted ski parkas, which were now sodden and heavy and useless for anything. For packs they had colorful contrivances from the discount department stores of Skokie or wherever they came from, with clevis pins made of plastic. One of the girls had lost a clevis pin, so that her pack was half off its frame.

"What's the Girl Scout motto?" asked one of my roommates from Lonesome. They were nice lads, but they might be pardoned for feeling just a little bit superior to this bobtail crew.

" 'Be prepared'?" said one of the matrons, a black-haired woman who was damp but undefeated. "No," she told him. "That's the *Boy Scout* motto. The Girl Scout motto is always to be able to find a Boy Scout." I took a clevis pin out of the bottom of the girl's pack and put it on top, where the strain was greater; I secured the bottom with a piece of string. (Like Dab Dab the Duck, no hiker should ever be without a piece of string.) Then I laid my trail map on the table for a conference with the matron. I showed her where she had started, where she now was, and why it was patently impossible that she could reach Mt. Washington in three days or even three weeks at the rate she was traveling. Next I showed her the Old Bridle Path and promised that if she would follow it downhill for a quarter of a mile, she would find a clearing where the girls could set up their tents.

"Eight tents?" she said.

"Well, maybe not eight. But couldn't you sleep three to a tent?"

"I suppose we could," she said. "You know, we've visited Washington, D.C., on this trip, and then we visited Gettysburg, but I really think this adventure is the best of all."

Right there, I decided that my daughter would never join the Girl Scouts. Any camping Kate does, she will do with me, at least until she is old enough to find a Boy Scout of her own.

In all of this, I must confess, my motives weren't entirely pure. Greenleaf Hut was already overbooked by five. If the Girl Scouts should decide to stay, they would have to sleep on the tables with me, and the common room of Greenleaf would in that case be a very damp place to spend the night. So I wanted to do anything in my power to ease their departure. They cleared out on schedule, ragtag and bobtail, hiking down the Old Bridle Path to the promised clearing.

After dinner, a tunafish casserole, I walked down to see how they were faring. I didn't have far to go. Their tents were pitched at crazy angles among the trees, not a hundred yards from the Greenleaf water tower. I asked them how they were getting along. Just fine, they said. They'd had Cup-a-Soup for dinner.

I walked back to the hostel, where the largest group of all—twenty-three students and faculty from a summer ecology seminar—were bird-watching on the rocks. Always eager to improve my education, I infiltrated them. One girl was wearing a T-shirt that said CONN in block letters, only on her they came out cursive. She claimed to have seen a green-throated warbler. Upon further questioning, it proved that the green-throated warbler (I think I have it right) was the only bird she could positively identify, not counting bluejays, chickadees, and pigeons.

One of the faculty members challenged her: "Are you sure you're not thinking of a *blue*-throated warbler?"

This was getting too technical for me, so I infiltrated other groups. In one, the subject was the weather. "I should have never taken this seminar," somebody said. "My first mountain and it had to rain."

"Yes," somebody agreed. "On a night like this, they ought to have a nice roaring wood fire."

But who would carry the nice wood up to the hut?

Here is another conversation I overheard that evening, while the cloud-fog boiled around Eagle Lake and sometimes obscured it altogether:

"When you stay in the huts you don't have to carry your own food, and that really takes the curse out of hiking. The other morning, after that wonderful bacon breakfast, we came out of the hut and saw two backpackers stirring up something—"

"Oatmeal?"

"Oatmeal or worse. I really felt sorry for them."

Wondering what this lady would have said to my plastic bags of pemmican, I wandered back to the ecology class. The students were looking at the mountain through binoculars. It was seven-thirty, and the great mass of Lafayette was clear at last, gray with rock and green with lichen, rising ponderously above Eagle Lake. (Eagle is no lake at all, but a weed-grown tarn that seemed distinctly smaller than it had last year. I judged that Greenleaf's water supply was in peril.) From the hostel, the trail dipped down through scrub to Eagle Lake, then climbed again to another and truer timberline. "There's somebody on the ridge!" the binocular people said. This announcement was greatly welcomed. The storm had passed and dinner with it, and there were few if any birds to be watched from Greenleaf Hut. But latecomers on the mountain—*that* was a diversion! Others came outside to look, including one of the hutboys. He stood in the time-honored posture of hutboys, hands-a-pocket beneath his apron.

People began to remember passing a family along the trail from Galehead Hut. Yes, and they hadn't been making very good time; yes, that was right, and wasn't there a six-year-old among them?

"Five hikers," the binocular people reported. "There's a boy in front, then a group of three, and the father is lagging behind. He's wearing a red jacket. Do you see it?"

Yes, I saw. My daughter was seven, and I wouldn't have taken her from Galehead Hut to Greenleaf in any kind of weather, never mind a day like this.

The students were thrilled. They began to assemble a rescue party: they would hike up to meet the stragglers; they would give them a hand with the packs; they would take flashlights in case they were a long time bringing them down.

"I hear an amateur," the hutboy said scornfully. "I hear someone who thinks a mountain rescue is *fun*."

But high fun it was for the students from Connecticut, and pretty soon there were more rescuers on the mountain than watchers at the hostel. The youngster in the lead didn't want to be rescued. He was eight, I would judge; he wore a yellow slicker and walked like a marionette, flat-footed and swaying from side to side, but he wouldn't give up his pack. He carried it all the way to the hostel, which he reached at eight o'clock, twelve hours exactly since he'd left Galehead that morning, having been drenched and fogbound and hailstoned along the way.

Then came mother, a girl about twelve, and the fabulous six-year-old. They had been willing to surrender their packs. Last of all came father, who was not so much the slowest as the wisest: he was in fine shape, after all. Unlike most people, including me, he apparently did not hurry when the world turned against him. He slowed down instead, which is by far the better thing to do.

The hutboys draped the kids in blankets. Then they prepared an eight-thirty dinner for the stragglers.

"David," said mother to the older boy, "can you wear this shirt?"

"No, it belongs to Mikey."

"I think it's yours."

"But Mikey always wears it."

"Listen, David, *it's yours.* Put it on!"

I think David was reluctant to give up his badge of honor, the gray AMC blanket he was wearing around his shoulders.

While mother was searching for dry garments, father was searching for dry cigarettes. He was a doctor, as it turned out. He told me that he'd done a lot of hiking with the older boy, but that this was the first time the whole family had gone on such an adventure.

"Would you do it again?" I asked.

"Sure," he said.

Father and I slept on the tables, because the men's bunkroom was overstocked with bodies. The bunks at Greenleaf were tiered four high and two wide; the aisles were very narrow, and of course there was a great quantity of wet clothing hanging about. I'd left my walking stick in the bunkroom. When I went in to retrieve it next morning, I decided that I'd been fortunate in my choice of sleeping arrangements.

Clivus multrum

It had been fourteen years since I last hiked to the summit of Lafayette. Then we'd scrambled more or less where we pleased. There were cairns to mark the general route, so we wouldn't lose our way, but otherwise the trail and the mountainside were one.

Now there was a beaten path to the summit. Lichen will not grow where too many Vibram soles have gone, so the Greenleaf Trail could be traced even from the hostel—a gray line upon the mountainside. When I followed it Thursday morning, I discovered that the trail crews had actually built stone walls at strategic points along the way. These barriers were subtle but real. Only the most determined wanderer would have taken the trouble to step over them; the rest of us walked exactly where the AMC has decided that we should walk.

There is a word for this process. Trails and campsites are "de-wildernized"—reduced to a more civilized condition—in the hope that the real wilderness will thereby remain untrammeled. The sensation is a bit like visiting the San Diego Zoo. You are standing in civilization, looking at a wilderness you cannot touch.

Yesterday at Greenleaf Hut, I'd met two interns from Pinkham Notch Camp. They were employed by the AMC research division, which studies such problems as water pollution and trail erosion, and which has a summertime staff of eight. This particular team was specializing in the Franconia Ridge. They would stretch a tape measure across the trail, hang a dropline from it, and record the depth and the type of soil or vegetation. This information was then compared to the "profile" taken a year ago at the same spot. As to the number of hikers who had caused the wear and tear, that information was also available: the AMC had concealed an electric eye on the Franconia Ridge Trail, between Lincoln and Lafayette. (I'd mentioned this fact to Thom Connelly. He vowed that he would find the counter and march back and forth in front of it for an hour.) The Franconia Ridge was chosen for this experiment because it is twice

vulnerable to erosion. It has a deep covering of soil, unlike most of the high ridges, and it is easier than most for the day hiker to reach. About ten thousand people passed this way in the summer of 1974.*

When I reached the summit of Lafayette, I understood why the AMC was sponsoring this study. The Franconia Ridge was marked by a ribbon of brown—dead soil and dying trees—all the way south to Mt. Lincoln. To the north, the Garfield Ridge was in much the same condition. It was a supertrailway, to use another AMC term, and it was one of the saddest things I have ever seen.

Yet the hikers have been kind to it: there were no tentsites hacked into the scrub, there were no orange peels or cigarette butts, and five feet off the trail the spruce and fir had a virgin look. It was only the footpath that had been ruined. Ten thousand hikers are twice too many.

I did a lot of humping on the Garfield Ridge. Some of this was serious enough to show on the map—three minor summits between Lafayette and Garfield—but more of it was the unrewarding up-and-down that had become so familiar on Monday and Tuesday. The morning was well spent before I came in sight of Garfield Pond. The water was just visible through the trees, its presence most clearly indicated by a bullfrog's *thump.*

When I last came this way, there had been a lean-to shelter at Garfield Pond. The month was October and the rain was dismal; for the first time in my mountain career I was unable to kindle a fire, so I chewed my dinner cold. It was a nice shelter for all of that. But it had since been demolished, a victim of the dewildernization program; the trail to the pond was now blocked by deadwood fences, and I had no great desire to bushwhack down to visit the old site.

It was a steep climb to the summit of Garfield, topping out at 4,488 feet. The summit was a devil's den of granite ledge, with a great concrete foundation which I took to be the base of a fire tower. I ate my lunch of pemmican and orange drink; most of the time I was above the clouds. They were swirling to the south, in the valleys that form the upper part of the Pemigewasset Wilderness; sometimes Owl's Head was visible and sometimes it was not. The same was true of Lafayette. It kept moving in and out of the clouds, as insubstantial as it was mighty. I was very happy. This was the fourth day of my hike, and I had never before tramped the White Mountains for more than a

---

The U.S. Forest Service also has a "backcountry research program." (For reasons to be explained later, the Forest Service does not like to say wilderness.) The government researchers are concentrating on a section of the Appalachian Trail as it passes from New Hampshire into Maine. Not one but six electric eyes have been installed there, in what is called the Mahoosuc Laboratory.

long weekend. The fourth day, I realized, is a very good day. The aches are gone, the pack is lighter, and the mind is accustomed to the new routine. So quickly are habits formed: I felt that I had been walking the mountains forever, that this was my duty and privilege in life.

In part, no doubt, my pleasure was physical. I had trained for this hike by swimming fifty laps a day and by walking long distances with a loaded pack, but the truth is that you cannot train for the mountains. The muscles are different. Swimming, jogging, and calisthenics: the muscles are different. The only thing that can prepare you for the Garfield Ridge Trail is the trail itself, and it is on the fourth day that everything comes together.

The downhill pitch was likewise steep, all the way to the side-trail that led to Garfield Ridge Campsite. There, in addition to a gurgling spring, I found a bridge that would have looked more at home in a Japanese garden. It was a busy intersection. Hikers were filling their canteens, rinsing their faces, or just loafing on the bridge.

Garfield Ridge Campsite is a fine example of the AMC's new program of dewildernization. It is several hundred feet from the trail, so that the campers are isolated from the hikers, and vice versa. It is designed for maximum use and minimum damage, with a shelter, tent platforms, a full-time caretaker, and a Clivus Multrum toilet. All of which—but especially the last—were reasons for me to spend an evening there. According to the *New Hampshire Times,* Clivus Multrum means "inclining compost room." I am thirty years removed from a Latin class and cannot vouch for the translation. However, I can report with confidence that Abby Rockefeller is the president of Clivus Multrum USA, that she sold thirty-five units in her first year in the business, that four of them were installed in New Hampshire, and that one of these may be viewed at Garfield Ridge Campsite. It cost $1,500 and was freighted into place beneath a helicopter.

You see, the pit toilet is a thing of the past in the White Mountains, except for a few isolated campsites. For a time the Forest Service and the AMC were able to shuffle the outhouses from place to place, one step ahead of a typhoid epidemic. Then they turned to the "crapper barrel" concept: fifty-five-gallon oil drums which are airlifted in and out at great expense. (The AMC figures that each time a hiker uses one of its crapper barrels, the cost to the club is twenty-five cents.) Thus the Clivus Multrum experiment, which could eliminate the airmail charges while providing useful fertilizer.

The toilet was invented in 1945 by a Swede named Rikard Lindstrom. It consists of a fiberglass chamber nine feet long and sloping toward the back, with three compartments and three openings. Human waste goes into the first of these, garbage and other organic material into the second. The third opening is a cleanout door. By the time the waste reaches this door—1,500 Swedes can't be wrong—it has been reduced to a compost that is odorless, rich in nutrients, and as clean as the soil that grows your daily vegetables.

The caretaker at Garfield Ridge Campsite was a young woman named Carol Varner. She lived in a green wall-tent that was strategically located beside the path, so that every visitor had to pass her door. She told me to make myself at home: she would come around later to collect my dollar. So I followed the path to the shelter (I couldn't have strayed if I wanted to, for there was a railing on each side of the path) and found that it was vastly different from the lean-tos I was accustomed to see in the White Mountains. It was too long by half, as indeed it had to be, since the traditional eight-man version was too small for the 1970s. This one slept twelve. The front was partially closed to keep the weather out. The top was covered with green roll-roofing, and the sides were those "log cabin" planks that are sometimes used for summer cottages, machine-rounded on the outside and flat on the inside. A pox on the AMC for that innovation. If a shelter cannot be built from logs, then it should be built from boards. Under no circumstances should it be built from boards masquerading as logs.

Carol Varner registers a guest, and collects a dollar, at the Garfield Campsite tent platforms

I unrolled my mattress and sleeping bag in the usual corner, where at most I would have just one person sleeping next to me. Then I went off to look for Clivus Multrum.

Unfortunately, Clivus was not yet operational. There was a padlock on the door and a polyethylene tarp over the composting chamber, and there was much building material about. I sought out Carol Varner. She told me that Clivus was delivered the previous fall, and that during the winter a curious hiker had pried open the cleanout door. One of her tasks this Thursday was to repair the damage with a fiberglass patch. Next she would install a vent pipe, a roof, and a composting base of straw and garbage. If I returned in a week or two, she said, I might have the privilege of being one of Clivus' first patrons.

"Will it work at this latitude?"

"It works in Sweden."

"Will it work at four thousand feet?"

"The composter does," she said, so we went to have a look at the composter.

Where the paths converged from the shelter, the tent platforms, and the latrines, the AMC had provided a pot-washing stand. This consisted of a galvanized bucket for large scraps of food, and a wire screen through which the campers were supposed to filter their wash water. Once a day Carol collected the garbage. She took it to a polyethylene composter—a miniature greenhouse—where it was left to rot. There is no smell from a functioning composter, and there was none from Carol's, nor were there any flies. This miracle was explained and illustrated in a display at the pot-washing center. "The sun and God's microbes do the rest," it declared, and at Garfield Ridge Campsite the theory was working just fine.

Another experiment that had proved itself was that campers would accept the presence of a caretaker. A lot depends on the caretaker, of course. Carol Varner was a friendly and efficient person who carried a satchel on her rounds, like a London bus conductor, except that hers was made of canvas. From it she produced, as the occasion demanded, a camping permit or the makings of a cigarette. She was the first woman I'd ever seen roll her own, and she was as competent at that as at everything else. The weed came out looking as if it had been factory made. There were none of the twisted ends, hollow places, or spilled tobacco that I remembered from World War Two, when my father had briefly flirted with Bull Durham.

Unlike most women employees of the AMC, Carol had not worked her way up from the kitchen at Pinkham Notch Camp. She had hiked the Appalachian Trail last year, which was apparently her main qualification for the job. (She earned college credit for the hike, incidentally. Carol was then a student at Hampshire College in Massachusetts, a new institution with new ideas, and by walking from Georgia to Maine she not only got independent-study credits toward a degree, but also saved herself considerable money on tuition, board, and room.) I asked if she'd seen Thom Connelly and Bobby Ramsey.

Yes, she said; they'd been here last night.

I went back to the lean-to and found that I had gained a companion. He was combing his hair—most unusual for a hiker. Then he bound it in a handkerchief, like Aunt Jemima, to keep the black flies away.

By God, he too was a Through Hiker. His name was Dave Stan; he'd graduated from the University of Virginia in June, a reserve second lieutenant with time on his hands, so he had decided to hike the Appalachian Trail while he waited for his call-up. Since it was so late in the season, Dave was heading south instead of north. This was not the best way to approach the Appalachian Trail. "In Maine sometimes," he told me, "I was up to my waist in mud. Luckily I was hiking with a friend at the time, so there was somebody to pull me out. It worked the other way, too. I pulled him out. And once he fell into a stream where the current was really moving along; the current dragged him under and his pack kept him there, and he would have drowned if I hadn't been with him."

Dave's kit was far more elaborate than Thom Connelly's. He was carrying a stove, one-pot meals from the supermarket, fresh clothes to wear in camp, a plastic tube tent, and a nylon hammock. When he was caught overnight without shelter, Dave would string the hammock between two trees, the tube tent enclosing it and supported by its own ridgepole of parachute cord. Then he would wriggle into the hammock and pull the tent over him like a sheet, securing it fore and aft with a clothespin. "If it's raining," he said, "I don't bother with my sleeping bag. I'd rather be cold one night than get my sleeping bag wet."

His regimen was like mine, only more drastic. He got up at first light, which was four-fifteen these days, and he was on the trail by five o'clock. That enabled him to cover ten miles or more by early afternoon, even in the mountains, and gave him several hours to rest, clean up, and write in his journal. I asked him if he was thinking of a book or magazine article. "No," he said. "There's been too much written about the Appalachian Trail already."

Through Hikers are a special breed, and among their traits is a fraternal loyalty. On the strength of Dave's membership in the fraternity (and on the strength of my acquaintance with him) we were invited for tea in the caretaker's tent. Most of the talk was about the trail, of course. Dave wanted to know what the toughest section was. Carol pondered this, then said: "The Whites." Dave seemed pleased to hear it, and so was I.

Carol told us there was a Through Hiker in his eighties coming north, a man named Ernie who recited poetry for his bed and board. "He knows all of that Alaskan poet," she said. "*The Cremation of Sam McGee*—who wrote it?"

"Robert Service," I said, having recently introduced my daughter to Sam McGee and Dangerous Dan McGrew.

"Yes, Robert Service," Carol said. "Well, this man can recite every-thing that Service ever wrote."

"I'll keep an eye out for him," Dave Stan said. "I expect I'll be hearing more about him as he gets closer."

Do you feel it? Do you sense the world of the Through Hiker, the lore that is passed on the wing from Springer Mountain to Mt. Katahdin?

Meanwhile other hikers were coming in, including a group of ten from a summer camp. They disappeared in the direction of the tent platforms and were not seen again. Other tenters walked by the shelter and likewise disappeared, and probably there were some I didn't even see. Garfield Ridge Campsite was designed to scatter its customers, even while restricting the damage they could do. I might as well have been spending the night at the old lean-to near Garfield Pond. The only people in view were Dave Stan and I, three hikers who seemed to be in their thirties and who probably were pro-fessional men from Boston, and two boys with boundless energy. Between rain showers, these last two ran up to the summit of Gar-field to catch the view that had been denied them when they first crossed over. They told me that they'd started from Franconia Notch this morning. They'd reached Greenleaf Hut just in time to eat left-over blueberry pancakes, and they hoped to repeat the trick next morning at Galehead Hut.

At all the hostels and campsites, I had found public-service adver-tisements from the AMC and the Forest Service. For example, there was the Carry In/Carry Out sign, admonishing the traveler to leave nothing behind him, and even to pick up what others had left. (Modern hikers are remarkably fastidious. They almost never drop anything along the trail, but their good intentions seem to weaken when they reach a campsite: "destination trash" is the new problem in the mountains.) The Garfield lean-to had one of these signs. It also had a register, raw material for an AMC survey, which called for a name and address, point of entry, destination, number in the party, and comments on the shelter. At Eliza Brook, where I'd first filled out one of these forms, I gave my destination as Crawford Notch. I wasn't sure that I was good for the whole distance. Now, in the glow of my fourth-day prowess, I signed myself as bound for Hastings, Maine. It was a good feeling, even if the entry seemed pale beneath Dave Stan's: bound for Georgia.

The shelter also had a mimeographed sheet that analyzed the AMC's expenses here and at another supervised campsite last summer.

According to the AMC research division, then, each of us was costing the organization thirty-two cents, over and above the dollar we had paid to Carol Varner. I asked Carol how the fee system had been greeted. Very well, she said; most hikers understood the need for a caretaker at campsites like this one, and were willing to part with a dollar for the privilege of sleeping here. This might seem self-evident to anyone who is *not* a backcountry hiker. But to most of us the whole idea of hiking is to get away from caretakers, fences, and the exchange of money. I was surprised that she had not experienced some outrage from her customers.

Carol did admit that she sometimes waived the one-dollar fee. It appeared that the most likely recipients of her forgiveness were Through Hikers, who seldom carry any more dollars than will pay for groceries and an occasional coin-op laundry.

This was the balance sheet:

Income

Overnight fees	$2,360

Expenses

Caretaker salaries	$ 765
Caretaker food and supplies	460
Sanitation	750
Communications and overhead	600
Depreciation	600
Total	$3,175

The last four thousand footer

Dave Stan failed to hit the trail at five next morning. No doubt he woke up, as I did, and returned to sleep when he discovered that rain was sheeting down. We stirred again at seven o'clock. The rain had stopped by then, so I wished Dave a good day and set off eastward. The trail was wet—wet, slippery, and in the clouds—and it continued that way for the two and one-half miles to Galehead Hut. The visibility from the outlooks was no more than a hundred feet. I was passing through a spirit world, where spruce trees vanished even as I was looking at them.

None of this seemed to daunt the two boys who had shared the lean-to with us last night. They passed me before I was well underway; and when I reached the hostel they were ready to move on again. Yes, they said, they had arrived in time for leftovers, and once again the fare had been blueberry pancakes. And no, they hadn't left any for me. I went inside the hostel and breakfasted on pemmican and orange drink. Scraps of cloud were drifting past the windows.

Galehead Hut takes its name from a nearby peak, which on my map was shown as having an altitude of 3,925 feet. However, the U.S. Geological Survey had just finished remapping the White Mountains, this time using satellite photography instead of surveyors' instruments, and several peaks had been adjusted up or down in consequence.* Among them was Galehead. When the new maps were ready, Galehead would have gained a hundred feet of altitude—making it an honest-to-goodness Four Thousand Footer, and posing an ethical problem for me. But before you can understand the problem, you must understand the Four Thousand Footer Club.

In 1957 the AMC published a list of the four-thousand-foot peaks in the White Mountains. This was not just a matter of reading elevations from the survey maps, for virtually every knob and hummock has been christened in the past three hundred years. Over in the Northern Presidentials, Mt. Adams has three lesser summits which are known as Sam Adams, John Quincy Adams, and Adams Four. Obviously these are not mountains in their own right. But what of the Tripyramids in the Waterville Valley area? As the name suggests, these are three witches' hats on a common ridgeline: having traversed the ridge, has a hiker climbed three mountains or just one?

The correct answer is two. The AMC decided that to qualify as a distinct mountain, the summit must rise two hundred feet above the col between it and a taller neighbor. North Tripyramid and Middle Tripyramid passed this test; South Tripyramid didn't. Neither did several other peaks with the requisite elevation. As published, the list contained forty-six names, ranging in size from Mt. Tecumseh (4,004 feet) to Mt. Washington (6,288 feet).

Mountains may or may not be immutable, but our perception of them is always subject to error. After Jeremy Belknap accompanied the first scientific expedition to Mt. Washington in 1784, he reported that the summit "was computed in round numbers at . . . nearly 10,000 feet above the level of the sea." In 1804 Nathaniel Bowditch knocked it down to 7,055 feet, and in 1816 Jacob Bigelow reduced it by another hundred feet or so. As recently as 1930, the exact altitude was still in doubt. The maps gave one figure, the railway another, and the government bench mark yet a third, and none of them was the 6,288 feet that we now take for granted.

The declared reason for this list was that it might help disperse the foot traffic in the White Mountains. To an AMC Old Boy—one who had tramped with rucksack and hobnailed boots before World War Two—the trails seemed congested by 1957. Then as now, most hikers stuck to the supertrailways in the Northern and Southern Presidentials and on the Franconia-Garfield ridgeline. By publicizing the Four Thousand Footers, the AMC reasoned, it could encourage hikers to visit some of the underused parts of the White Mountains. Indeed, several of the listed peaks were outside the boundaries of the national forest.

There was another motive, too. There always is. Hikers are human, and humankind is obsessed with notions of achievement. To bag the Four Thousand Footers would be the equivalent of earning a varsity sweater, the Combat Infantryman's Badge, or whatever symbol of excellence might excite your admiration.

Since I do not belong to the AMC, the Four Thousand Footer Club remained unknown to me until 1962. Then, one fine September weekend, I hiked up the Ammonoosuc Ravine Trail to spend the night at Lakes of the Clouds Hut, on the south flank of Mt. Washington. After dinner I climbed a pinnacle a few hundred yards from the hostel—everyone else was climbing it, so I went along. Next morning I hiked to the summit of Mt. Washington and returned to the valley by a different route. I thought no more about it until, later in the week, I thumbed through the *AMC White Mountain Guide* and discovered the list. I realized that my after-dinner stroll had been to the summit of Mt. Monroe, 5,385 feet above sea level and 335 feet above the hut, and therefore a bona fide Four Thousand Footer. I had climbed two of the taller mountains in New Hampshire. Forty-four more and I could earn a shoulder patch.

I walked the White Mountains for the next four years, bagging summits where and when I could. I even made winter ascents, though that was not part of my program. (I didn't know that there was a subclub for those who had done the Four Thousand Footers in the winter.) One sunny December day, feeling restless at mid-morning, I jumped into my car and raced the clock to Franconia Notch; I reached it by noon, climbed Cannon Mountain in the snow, ran a dry slalom down the ski slopes, and returned home in time for dinner.

Early on, I enlisted a lawyer and a realtor as hiking companions. We were a fairly typical group for the time. In the 1960s, almost all hikers were Boy Scouts, professional men in their thirties or forties, or knotty-thighed oldsters from the AMC. You seldom met a hiker between the ages of sixteen and thirty. Now this age group overwhelms all others. Anyhow, we three did most of the major summits together, building campfires and cutting bough beds wherever we went, and always with a small bottle of whiskey. But the lawyer and the realtor failed me when it came to the minor Four Thousand

75

Footers. They weren't peak-baggers at heart.

Few people will admit to being peak-baggers. It is not a subject for boasting, just as no soldier will admit that he *wants* a Combat Infantryman's Badge. However, if you spend enough time in somebody's company you will discover his secrets one by one. Thus I learned that a married couple of long acquaintance, Norman and Priscilla by name, were also bagging the Four Thousand Footers. Since I had begun with the tallest and they with the lowest mountains, our lists were quite dissimilar. Nevertheless we had a number of unclimbed peaks in common, and we climbed those together. We also pledged to save one of them for last, so that we would all join the club together.

The final target was Owl's Head, a wooded mountain which stands alone in the upper part of the Pemigewasset Wilderness, eight miles from the Kancamagus Highway. Priscilla was not a strong hiker, so we decided to make a three-day trip of it: one day for walking in, another for climbing Owl's Head, and the third for returning to the highway. I had three bottles of champagne in my rucksack, with which to toast the last of the Four Thousand Footers. This was a heavy load, and the rucksack was venerable; the backband came apart before we reached our campsite. I had to carry the pack in my arms for the last mile or two. Like the rucksack, my self-esteem was badly frayed by this time. I realized that I was no longer hiking for the joy of it, but for the sole purpose of finishing that list.

We had talked about this problem before. Norman had even suggested that we stop within arm's reach of the final summit, slowly reach for the cairn, then *pull back*. Of course we didn't do it. It would have been impossible anyhow, because Owl's Head is so flat that the summit was wrongly marked for several years. Only a caterpillar could have bellied up to the cairn without actually standing above it. So we touched the damned thing, and Norman and Priscilla went ahead and made application for the next session of the Four Thousand Footer Club. I didn't. I was so disenchanted with myself that I sent my valiant rucksack to the dump, burned my copy of the AMC Guide, and did not walk the mountains again for four or five years.

Norman must have felt a similar emotion, because he didn't show me the patch he had earned. Come to think of it, I have never seen the famous shoulder patch. Does every member of the Four Thousand Footer Club feel the same way?

"It was awful," Norman confessed after returning from Boston. "The minute we went through the door, we knew what it would be like. There were *two dogs* in the auditorium, and they were wearing packs." Sure enough, the dogs were initiated with Norman, Priscilla, and 120 others. But what really distressed him was the discovery that two more lists had been compiled while we were finishing the first. These were the New England Four Thousand Footers (the original forty-six plus twelve in Maine and five in Vermont) and the Hundred

I once wrote a magazine article about the Four Thousand Footer phenomenon, doing most of my research in back copies of *Appalachia*. I found that the AMC ran its first peak-bagging expedition in 1957. Twenty members qualified that year, receiving their shoulder patches at the spring meeting in 1958. Patches were also awarded to the two charter members of the Four Thousand Footer Club—one of them posthumously—who had climbed the peaks a generation before.

The first winter ascents were made by a couple who lived in Randolph, New Hampshire. They finished the list by climbing Mt. Jefferson just before Christmas in 1961. Both were septuagenarians at the time.

The first dog to qualify for membership was a mongrel named Friskie, in 1963.

The youngest person to finish the list was a seven-year-old, also in 1963. (In fact, I think the seven-year-old was Friskie's owner, but I am not sure of this.)

And the eldest was a lady who finished the list in 1965, her eightieth year.

By 1967 the Four Thousand Footer Club was beginning to overwhelm its parent. From a pleasant interlude at the AMC annual meeting, the initiation rites had come to dominate the affair, so they were moved to a rented auditorium. The membership by this time included 462 humans and four dogs. Among the former were Norman and Priscilla, and it was quite a jolt to see their names in *Appalachia*. I was rushed with memories: turning back from Mt. Adams in a blizzard, spilling chicken casserole into the fire en route to the Hancocks, carrying my rucksack under my arm as we departed from Owl's Head. . . . For a moment, I wished that my name was on the list with theirs.

In recent years, the AMC has ceased to publicize the Four Thousand Footer Club. When I called the headquarters on Joy Street, I was referred to a man in Arlington, the current chairman of the Four Thousand Footer Club. He told me that the membership was almost two thousand and that it was growing at the rate of two hundred names a year.

"How many dogs?" I asked.

"My predecessor didn't care for dogs," the chairman said. "He refused to keep a separate list. Now it's impossible to go back through the records and determine which are dogs and which are people."

Then he had a surprise for me: Galehead had been promoted to a Four Thousand Footer.

"But that's impossible," I said.

"Not at all," he said. "The new maps are being prepared, and Galehead is a Four Thousand Footer. There will be a grace period, of course. Anybody who applies after that period must have Galehead on his list." Those who already had their patches, or who could apply forthwith, would be forgiven Galehead. A similar courtesy had been extended to the early climbers of Owl's Head, when the AMC realized that the true summit was several hundred yards from the cairn that was supposed to mark it.

Well, forgiveness was fine for the shoulder-patch brigade. But what of the ghost battalion—a considerable force, I suspect—those of us who bagged the peaks and then declined the reward? Were we obligated to return to the Garfield Ridge and take the side-trail to Galehead?

I thought so, and that was what brought me to Galehead Hut this Friday morning.

I asked the hutboy if I could leave my pack in the common room. He nodded without raising his eyes from his paperback novel. So I left my pack, but took my walking stick and windbreaker, and I set off to ascend my forty-seventh Four Thousand Footer. Clearly I was in the vanguard of Galehead-baggers. The side-trail was narrow and overgrown with shrubs—not at all like the well-trodden routes that had led me to the other Four Thousand Footers, even those that were still classified as bushwhacks when I climbed them. Take Mt. Tom, for example. Nobody bothered with Mt. Tom before 1957, and therefore it was without an official trail to the summit. By the time I reached it, however, enough peak-baggers had gone that way to trample a wide path through the trees. But on Galehead I was bushwhacking indeed, and every bush was dewdropped with rain. My jeans were soaked by the time I'd covered the half-mile to the summit. That was forgotten—all the silliness of the Four Thousand Footer Club was forgotten—when I stood on the summit cairn and admired the view.

The view mightn't have been worth the trouble on an ordinary day, but this day was far from ordinary. The cloud-fog was ripping past me, borne upward on the currents flowing from the Pemigewasset Wilderness. It was like the steam from a witch's cauldron, with the Garfield Ridge serving as its brim. Ghostly doings, spirits writhing, fleeing skyward from the pit. . . . The effect was almost terrifying. Standing there on the topmost rock, I though of Ahab obsessed with the white whale: *Talk not to me of blasphemy, man; I'd strike the sun if it insulted me.*

The random backpackers

Back at Galehead Hut, I bought three chocolate bars to supplement my pemmican. It hadn't occurred to me that the hostels would sell trail snacks, but most of them did, and what was more they sold them at the standard retail price. The hutboy had to put down his paperback while he attended to the sale. The book was *Jaws*. As long as I had his attention, I asked if he'd seen Thom Connelly and Bobby Ramsey yesterday morning. "Through Hikers?" he said. "Nah. They're a dime a dozen around here."

  "Do you have a register?"

"Haven't been able to get one," he said.

I left him to *Jaws.*

The next summit easterly was the pyramid known as South Twin. It deserves a richer name. When viewed from the south it is a perfect cone, like Fujiyama in the prints, and from any direction the climb to its summit is enough to keep a strong man out of trouble for the better part of an hour. At the top, I met three hikers bound for Galehead Hut. "You'll arrive in time for lunch," I told them, "but I can't promise that the hutboy will be happy to see you." They said that they belonged to a hiking club from Toronto, that they numbered twenty-three all told, and that they were doing the huts from Carter Notch to Greenleaf.

For the next hour, down into the col and up again to Mt. Guyot, I kept meeting Canadians. They were an oddly matched group, all ages and all speeds, and I don't think I saw all of them. I lost count after the third or fourth meeting.

Somewhere along the trail, I also met a spruce grouse. She was a fat, speckled hen, and she trotted three paces in front of me for a hundred yards or more, until she saw the next group of Canadians and scooted off into the undergrowth. She was the largest wild creature I had seen since leaving home. That is an odd feature of wilderness travel: you don't see much wildlife. I live on the very edge of the Great Eastern Seaboard Shopping Mall, but there are more creatures in those woods than I have ever seen in the White Mountains. It's a rare day that I do not encounter a raccoon at least, or a rabbit or white-tail deer; in season there are grouse, hawk, pheasant, and even a great blue heron down on the marsh. Perhaps, like us, they have grown accustomed to noise and motion, losing some of their wildness as the Shopping Mall creeps nearer. Whereas the mountain creatures still shun the paths that men have made.

Mt. Guyot is a great sprawl of a mountain, where two ridges meet in *T* formation. The Appalachian Trail passes north of the summit. I would leave the AT here, heading south into the lowlands of the Pemigewasset Wilderness, and would not see the familiar white blazes again until I reached Mt. Washington in six days' time.

I was at the intersection by noon. The day was brighter now, but still cool, and the cloud-fog was still rolling across the ridgeline. The stately hump of Guyot was visible from time to time; the trail was likewise visible, a barren line through the scrub that looked like juniper but was actually dwarf spruce and fir. I hunkered down among the rocks to eat my lunch. Then I smoked a cigarette. Three matches were needed to light the thing: my supply was getting damp, and I decided to replace paper matches with wooden ones when I passed through Crawford Notch. It was a splendid place to contemplate the trail ahead. There was no one in view—no Canadians straggling from the east, nobody on the trail from Guyot, nobody toiling up the Twinway behind me. At that moment, the backpacker explosion seemed vastly overrated. I was at Bondcliff Junction on the Appalachian Trail, and there was nobody in sight but me. It struck me, too, that if I'd followed that brown speckled hen into the undergrowth, I might in a very few feet have been standing where no human being had ever stood before.

Following the line of cairns to Guyot summit was, I think, the happiest moment of my hike. The day's walk was nearly over, my pack and staff had become a part of me, and I was surrounded by the wild splendor of rock, scrub, and wind-blown fog. I felt like the hero of an Irish ballad.

Guyot Shelter was as I had remembered it from my last visit, not a lean-to but a little house open at the front, with a lower deck of earth and an upper deck of squared-off logs. It was a very special shelter, not only in its design but in its view as well. It faced east. The mountains rolled away, one behind the other graying as they went, all the way to Montalban Ridge, the ten-mile-long buttress of Mt. Washington. Nearer at hand were Mt. Willey and the other peaks that formed the walls of Crawford Notch. Nearer still was the great bare slab of Whitewall at Zealand Notch; nearest of all, a strange extension of Mt. Bond where no trees could grow, thanks to the severity of the winds that blew across it. All this I remembered from 1965, when I had stayed at Guyot Shelter with the lawyer, the realtor, and a young woman who intended to become the first barefoot member of the Four Thousand Footer Club.

Everything else was different. Even the access trail had been relocated, because the old path was too close to the brook that was the water supply. The new path was farther north. It led steeply down to the green wall-tent on a wooden platform that I was learning to recognize as the mark of a supervised campsite. This one was equipped with a small sundeck and a rough-sawn rocking chair, from which the caretaker could admire the view.

The caretaker was Frank Vitale, bushy-bearded, bushy-haired, a hulking but gentle man who impressed me as more of a woodsman than a backpacker. No doubt the impression came from his insect repellent, which was the infamous Old Woodsman's Fly Dope—100 percent active ingredients, and each ingredient with a reek of its own. Frank laved his hands and face with it. Then he would take off his wool cap (it had once been pink) and squirt it generously with dope.

"Actually," he told me, "real woodsmen don't use this stuff. They use Vicks Vaporub. You go into one of those logging camps and it smells like an infirmary."

He was building a new tent platform when I arrived. Materials for the campsite had been helicoptered to Guyot summit, Frank told me, and had then been packed down the mountainside. There was no place on this steep and wooded slope for a helicopter to land. He also told me that the shelter would soon be replaced by a new one, probably on the Garfield model.

To be sure, Guyot Shelter was showing its age. It had begun to droop towards the front, which would oblige me to sleep with my head at the back wall. This seemed to be the customary practice: almost every camper on this trip had slept with his feet to the front and his head to the rear. I preferred to sleep the other way. Not to see the stars, for there were none these cloudy nights, but to reinforce the notion that I was in the wilderness. At Guyot Shelter, if I didn't want to have my feet higher than my head, I would have to follow the general rule. I unrolled my little mattress, took my sleeping bag out of its sack, and put all my spare clothes in the sack for a pillow. This I moored to the mattress with the same ties which kept it from unrolling during the day. I would be glad to have that mattress tonight. On my last visit to Guyot Shelter, the corduroy deck had been cushioned by successive layers of spruce boughs, from gray dust to brown skeletons to fresh and fragrant green.

Soon I had company: four boys and two counselors from a summer camp. There was something unusual about that ratio. I'd often met summer-camp groups in the mountains, but never a group that was so closely supervised. One counselor for four or five hikers was more like it.

The boys were unusual, too. They were extraordinarily handy with knives, conjuring the blades from their pockets and sticking them into the logs of the shelter. This is more difficult than the movies would have you believe. Like the ability to make a bank shot in pool, it is one of the signs of a misspent youth.

Guyot Shelter had an advertised capacity of twelve, but somehow the boys managed to fill it completely, two on the ground and two on the upper deck with me. They spread tent-flys and clothing to dry. They poked my pack, hefted my walking stick, and inspected my gear, boundlessly curious about everything. Then they bummed one of my cigarettes and went behind the shelter to smoke it. I could hear their voices:

"I should have stolen more. Then I'd be better off."

"Hah. If you hadn't stolen so much, you wouldn't be here."

The counselors decided to pitch a tent at one of the platforms. They told me that they were from an outfit called Random Backpacking, which specialized in kids from the Boston area. And not just any kids, either, but those who had run afoul of the juvenile courts. My four shelter-mates were doing time. Instead of sending them to a training school, the courts had sentenced them to a summer in the White Mountains under the aegis of Random Backpacking. The cost—sixty dollars a week—was paid by a grant from the U.S. government. It seemed like a bargain all around. No reform school was ever built that could operate on sixty dollars a week per juvenile; and the kids were getting an experience modeled on that of Outward Bound, which costs five times as much.

They had been walking three days in the rain through the Pemigewasset Wilderness. Today they'd come up the Bondcliff Trail from Camp Sixteen—five hours of hard slogging, the counselors told me. This was not the best news they could have brought. My program for tomorrow included that same trek to Camp Sixteen, only in the reverse direction, then an additional five miles to Desolation Shelter. Nor could I modify it. There was no shelter at Camp Sixteen, and anyhow I couldn't spare an extra day: Sally expected to see me on Sunday afternoon in Crawford Notch, the day after tomorrow. I resolved to follow Dave Stan's regime. I would get up at first light and tackle Mt. Bond before breakfast.

Meanwhile the Random Backpackers had returned from their forbidden cigarette. They would be walking north to US 3 tomorrow, over South and North Twin, and they debated whether the van would be there to take them home. They invented excuses for the driver. If the van had crashed and the driver was dead, that would be an acceptable excuse; if he were hospitalized, they might or might not forgive him, depending on the extent of his injuries; but any lesser accident would not do.

If the van wasn't there, they decided, they would employ their "group resources," which I took to mean that they would steal a car.

The boys then hunted up some deadwood and began to jump on it, trying to smash it into kindling. One of the counselors put a stop to this activity. I admired his style: "Why don't you go up and ask the caretaker if it's all right to build a fire?"

"Talk about passing the buck," I said to the counselor, a roly-poly youngster with grandma glasses, not too far removed from the juvenile courts himself. He winked at me.

Frank Vitale came down the trail with a cardboard box full of firewood. While he set the fire, he gave a lecture that was no lecture, but an uncle's good advice. "If we burn the deadwood around the shelter," he explained, "we get what we call a 'human browse line.' There won't be anything in sight, as high as a man can reach and out for a quarter-mile around. So what I do, I take my packboard and I go down into the woods and I cut firewood for people who need it." Actually, the Random Backpackers didn't need the wood—they had a gasoline stove—but Frank clearly felt that the lesson was worth a few sticks of wood. "And this piece," he said, "is like the little fish that you throw back into the river." He picked up the deadwood the boys had found, and he threw it over the railing. In Frank's view, even a dead branch was part of the living world.

One of the boys was staring at him in wonder. "You're the caretaker here?" he asked at last.

"Yes," Frank said.

"Well, what kind of a job is that?"

Frank pushed his once-pink cap to the back of his head. Patiently he went through it again: his job was to keep Guyot Campsite from becoming an eyesore. Every few weeks, he explained, he would pack out the non-burnable rubbish, eggshells especially, and the aluminum-foil wrappers from cigarette packages, supermarket foods, and even the freeze-dried meals that were sold by mountain specialty firms. A typical week's accumulation of this rubbish was ten or fifteen pounds, and this despite the fact that Frank was there to encourage better behavior.

"Oh yeah," the boy said. "*That.*"

I'll say this for Random Backpacking: they ate well. They had several cans of Dinty Moore's Beef Stew, which they improved with rice, fresh celery and carrots, and packaged gravy mix. The stew was so bountiful that the counselors sent offerings to the tent platforms back in the woods.

I took two servings of this glorious mixture, my first hot food of the day. Then I went back to the shelter with the intention of sleeping nine hours. I was interrupted once by an argument from the ground floor; it went on for some time, but finally was silenced by one of the boys on the upper deck with me. "Hey, hey," he called softly.

"What?" said a voice from the ground floor.

"Shut up, why dontcha?"

There was a silence. Then the ground floor replied: "Hey, take it easy, why dontcha?" But they took the request in a friendly spirit, concluded their argument, and went to sleep.

Henry's woods

I was on the trail by five o'clock, and on the summit of Mt. Bond by six. There I had breakfast under a threatening sky, but one tall enough to show me the world. There was no cloud-fog in the Pemigewasset Wilderness this morning.

The summit of Mt. Bond is a special place: of all the White Mountains, it is the one farthest removed from civilization. From my breakfast nook I could see the multiple ridges that I had admired yesterday from Guyot Shelter, plus a little more. Southeast rose the Hancocks, twin mountains in a rolling hardwood forest, with the brown line of the East Branch snaking through. Due south, the hardwood forest was interrupted by the Bondcliffs, ragged and mighty, the last high ground I would traverse before dropping down into the Pemigewasset Wilderness. And to the west and north was the great horseshoe ridge I had walked yesterday and the day before, from Mt. Lafayette to Mt. Garfield and the pyramid of South Twin. The last of these, as I have already said, looked like Fujiyama's cone in the light of morning.

So I was cupped in an immense bowl of mountains, and though I was sitting on one of the taller peaks, nevertheless I had the distinct impression that the horizon was taller still. I remembered reading about this phenomenon in my grade-school years, when I had devoured the prose of Richard Halliburton and Ralph Paine and all the men who had journeyed to far places and written about them. One of these adventurers had climbed an isolated peak—in South America, I think—and had remarked that no matter how high he climbed, the horizon climbed with him. No mountaineer can stand above the horizon. So, for all practical purposes, one summit will do as well as the next. The need is only to be on a mountaintop, whether it be Bond at 4,700 feet or Everest at 29,000. *And not to see a highway anywhere.*

The Pemigewasset Wilderness got its name because it is drained by the East Branch of the Pemi; and because, one hundred years ago, it was a wilderness indeed. The Appalachian Mountain Club was founded in 1876. One of its projects was to publish a magazine called *Appalachia,* and the first issue referred to the East Branch country as an area in need of "exploration." Probably the first party to accept the challenge was an AMC group from Boston. They came this way in 1883, passing over Mt. Bond and the Bondcliffs and so to the Pemigewasset Wilderness.

By 1890, however, loggers had discovered the Pemi. It was, as C. Francis Belcher later described it in *Appalachia,* "a virgin paradise full of fish, animals and adventure . . . its valleys were deeper and wider, its shoulders broader and richer, and its spruce and fir as well-aged and full of board feet as any other land unit in these hills."

There is precious little spruce and fir in the Pemi now. The loggers took most of it, clearcutting 35,000 acres between 1893 and 1907. By the end of this miniscule era, there was nothing but slash in the valleys and on the lower slopes. All that was required to start it burning was a lightning strike or a spark from a locomotive. This was provided in August of 1907. "Following the lumberman comes the fire," editorialized the Boston *Globe* on August 27. "Survey from Mt. Lafayette shows Mt. Bond to be swept clean, the easterly slope of Mt. Garfield burned over, and the southerly slope of Mt. Guyot fiercely burning with flames eating up Mt. Lafavette."

The fire raged for ten days. It caused a popular revulsion against the loggers, and led in a very few years to the creation of the White Mountain National Forest. Ironically, the Pemi itself was not set aside for another generation. Latter-day loggers were still picking it over, like carrion crows, when I first drove around the mountains after World War Two. It was not until 1948 that the last tracks were lifted from the East Branch and Lincoln Railroad, which at the height of its glory had carried three trains a day from the cuttings, each laden with seven thousand board feet of timber.

Most of the Pemi, then, is second-growth hardwoods. The spruce is beginning to come back, and there is primeval growth on some of the more inaccessible slopes; but the view from Mt. Bond is a broad-leafed forest such as can be seen in southern New Hampshire, where the farms were abandoned during the Great Depression. The Pemi is beautiful, especially in the autumn, but it is not the wilderness it was in the 1880s.

That is why the U.S. Forest Service refuses to honor the popular name. Names are very important to bureaucrats; if you call something *wilderness* you might find yourself obliged to manage it as such, meaning that no roads can be built through it, no timber cut, and no motorcycles or snowmobiles allowed on its trails. To avoid this possibility, the Forest Service calls this place the Pemigewasset Unit.

In the six o'clock haze, at the upside-down treeline on Mt. Bond, the Pemi looks like wilderness indeed

91

Even the Appalachian Mountain Club has been swayed by this logic. Since 1969, AMC maps and publications have referred to the Pemigewasset "Wilderness"—like that, in quotation marks—as if to emphasize that the Pemi lost its virginity long ago.

Better that they should have renamed it altogether. "Henry's Woods" would be as good a name as any. That is what the Pemi was commonly called at the turn of the century, in tribute to James Everell Henry, the man who cut it clean.

While I was thinking these grand thoughts atop Mt. Bond, the first drops of rain began to fall. I took out my poncho and wrapped it around the pack. The rain wasn't serious enough to trouble the rest of me, but I wanted to keep my duffel dry. Then I set out for Henry's Woods. As I descended the south slope of Mt. Bond, I went from man-high trees to scrub and finally to bare rock, reaching "treeline" at about four thousand feet. On this exposure—thanks to the freakish winds that swirled up from the Pemi—Bond was an upside-down mountain. The higher elevation was wooded; the lower elevation was bare.

Ahead of me on the Bondcliffs—man against the sky!—I saw another hiker. I was astonished to see anyone so early in the day. I wasn't sure what time it was, since on Mt. Bond I had attempted to wind Sally's watch while the stem was out, and I had sent the hand spinning around the dial. But I didn't think it was as late as seven. If the hikers (two of them, as I saw when we drew closer) had come from Camp Sixteen, they were moving very fast indeed.

They proved to be middle-aged men in day packs. And they hadn't come from Camp Sixteen but from the Kancamagus Highway, nearly nine miles away. The time, they said, was six forty-five. I wanted to know more about their trail technique—had they carried torches or had they run, to get here so early?—but their minds were fixed on the mountains ahead. "How far is Guyot?" they wanted to know. "Five miles?"

"Oh no. Two or three at the most." I pointed out the trail. "Mt. Bond is straight ahead. You won't go over that other summit—that's West Bond—unless you're bagging peaks."

"Oh, we'll get it," they said, with the joy of hunters who had seen a fine stag. "We plan to get six today."

So they were doing the Four Thousand Footers. I wished them well and began the short climb to the cliffs. In a storm more serious than this one, the Bondcliff Trail would have been a terror along here. The trail in places was an arm's length from the cliffs, and the drop to the west was five hundred feet sheer, then a more gentle five hundred feet to Hellgate Brook. I wouldn't have cared to time the fall to Hellgate, and I was glad that on this Saturday the clouds were high above me.

After the cliffs, the trail descends sharply to Camp Sixteen, follow-ing the course of Black Brook. The AMC Guide warned me that there are eight crossings of this stream, and that some of them were hard to find, especially on the descent. I decided to fix the crossings in my mind. After I was well into the hardwoods, I made a little tent from my poncho, staff, and two convenient saplings. While doing so, I heard someone whistling on the upward path. He jumped when I said hello. "My God, you scared me," he said. "I didn't expect to meet anyone on the trail this morning."

I liked him immediately, no doubt because his style was the same as mine: he walked alone, he wore long pants, and he carried a full-sized walking stick. I can understand why most hikers prefer to flock together. Solo hiking isn't exactly dangerous, but it does increase the anxiety level at times—in stormy weather especially, or when the trail proves longer or more obscure than its description in the AMC Guide. Then it's a boon to have companionship. But why do so many hikers expose their legs to every thorn and black fly in the area? And why do so few of them carry walking sticks? Not a yard-long branch picked up along the trail, either, but a staff carefully whittled from ash or other resilient hardwood. It serves as tent pole, clothes line, raccoon-chaser, and infallible third leg in difficult terrain, and best of all it never argues about the route you have chosen.

We talked for a while, the solo hiker and I. He'd spent the night at Camp Sixteen, and he reported that the brook crossings were no great problem.

Nor were they, after I folded my tent and started for the lowlands. It was raining steadily by the time I made the eighth crossing. I was wearing the poncho now, instead of just draping it over my pack, and the raindrops were snapping against the plastic like a multitude of rubber bands. The ground was level here. The trees were young hard-woods, their foliage jungle-green and hanging almost straight with their burden of water. And in the middle of the path I saw—*memento mori*—a length of track from the East Branch and Lincoln Railroad. The rail was black and gleaming in the rain, overlooked somehow when the tracks had been taken up and scrapped.

J.E. Henry built that railroad. "I never saw the tree yet," he once said, "that didn't mean a damned sight more to me going under the saw than it did standing on a mountain."

He arrived in Lincoln in 1892. He created the town and owned it: the sawmill that was its reason for being, the millworkers' houses, the hospital, the hotel, the store, the generating plant, the icehouse, and of course the East Branch and Lincoln Railroad. J.E. Henry was the judge. His son John was the postmaster. The company store sold everything the workers required, except alcohol, and that was forbidden because it interfered with work. Immigrant laborers were given free transportation from Boston. On the back of their tickets were these words: "Lincoln, N.H., is one mile from the town of North Woodstock on the Concord & Montreal Railroad. It is the headquarters of the J.E. Henry & Sons Lumber Co., one of the largest firms in the state. A good man can find work all year. A poor man better not go there, as such men are not wanted."

The East Branch and Lincoln Railroad was built in segments. The track followed the cuttings, with the camps numbered in sequence as the line moved east from Lincoln, first along the site of the present Kancamagus Highway, later moving into the northern valleys.

Camp Sixteen, early in this century, was a community of 150 woodcutters, their horses, and their teamsters and foremen, all housed in buildings fourteen feet wide and between thirty and forty feet long. When the cutting was exhausted, the buildings were moved by rail to the next camp. Among his other accomplishments, therefore, J.E. Henry must be credited with constructing the first mobile homes.

Now there were six or seven tents between the trees, blue and red, the homes of a new breed of woods-gypsy. I went over to say hello. The tents were pitched on wooden platforms provided by the Forest Service. (Until 1972, there was a lean-to shelter at Camp Sixteen, but it burned that year and was not replaced.) The tenters were staying for the day, hoping that the rain would stop before Sunday required them to go home. They were weekenders for the most part: they had hiked in last night and would hike out again tomorrow. The Pemi is very popular with weekenders because the walking is so easy, the trails straight and level where J.E. Henry laid the tracks of his railroad.

I hunkered beneath my poncho for a ten o'clock lunch. Then I turned east on the Wilderness Trail, thinking what a glorious ski route it would be. I was joining the trail at its halfway point: it begins at the Kancamagus Highway and follows the river and the railroad bed for nine miles to Stillwater Junction, where the East Branch has its source in three small tributary streams.

For years I'd wanted to make a ski traverse of the Pemi, entering by way of the Zealand Road to the north. The first day would be an easy six miles to the AMC's Zealand Falls Hut. I would ski out through Zealand Notch on the second day, pick up the Thoreau Falls Trail, and so to the highway along the trail I was now walking—thirteen miles altogether, and almost all of it a gentle downhill run. I was full of this dream when I met a hiker and his two young sons. "What a ski trail," I said, unmindful of how this must have sounded on a rainy morning in July.

The father looked at me sideways. "Ayuh," he agreed. "That's what they use it for in the win*tuh*." Either he was from Maine or he was making fun of me.

They'd come from Desolation Shelter, and yes, the lean-to had been crowded last night. I thanked them and moved on.

Half a mile from Camp Sixteen, the railroad bed crosses to the south bank of the river, and the Wilderness Trail crosses with it. The East Branch here is quite a river, draining as it does the entire northeast quadrant of the Pemi. Until 1959 hikers make the crossing on the old railroad trestle, but the Forest Service decided that it was unsafe and built a 180-foot suspension bridge for our exclusive use. It bounced and swayed beneath my footsteps. Off to the right, old No. 17 Trestle was a solid mass of timbers. I would have preferred to be walking on them, despite the warnings posted at either end.

Then I was back on the railroad bed, in an avenue about twenty feet wide, and gently climbing through the hardwoods. The crossties were still in place, still square and solid after seventy-five years. They were hemlock—cut in the Pemi, milled in Lincoln—and not a drop of preservative had ever been applied to them. They looked good for another seventy-five years, thanks to the skill with which the railroad had been laid and drained. "Anywhere east of Lincoln is rough, tough engineering country," Francis Belcher pointed out in *Appalachia*, "and it is a lasting tribute to the seldom well-educated civil engineers of Henry & Co., that their handiwork will be evident throughout the upper Pemigewasset valleys for many years to come." The most notable of these engineers was a certain Levi Dumas, who was so stout that he was commonly known as Pork Barrel. He could write his name and read it too, but that was the limit of his schooling. Pork Barrel Dumas gets the credit for the dryness of the Wilderness Trail, for the solidity of No. 17 Trestle, and for the ingenious buildings that once occupied Camp Sixteen. And he was indirectly responsible for the absence of sharp turns on the EB&L. The railroad had to be straight and wide, so that the buildings could be moved from one camp to the next.

These camps were so heavily trammeled that most of them are still open. The next clearing to the eastward was Camp Eighteen, grown to grass and a wildflower that reminded me of hollyhocks, but without so much as a sapling to indicate the passage of time. It might have been abandoned last year. I passed a rusty metal bucket beside the trail, in which hikers had carefully deposited their trash. I also found a panel from a cast-iron stove, modestly Victorian in its design.

I was plodding now, picking up my boots and setting them down as if they too had been cast from iron. Four miles over the Bondcliffs. Then five miles along the Wilderness Trail. At last I crossed the East Branch on a crib of logs and brush, followed a recently cut path through the woods, and came in time to Stillwater Junction. Here the Wilderness Trail ended. I took the right fork to Desolation Shelter, which I reached at one o'clock.

Three young lads were already in residence. They explained that they had reached the lean-to yesterday, too late to find space inside, so they had spent the night in a plastic tent like the one I was carrying. It had split during the night. So they had moved into the shelter after breakfast, too damp and discouraged to go anywhere today.

The Desolation region was named by the woodcutters themselves: even they were awed by the wasteland they had created. But nature has healing powers beyond the understanding of the average wood-cutter, and certainly beyond the understanding of most ecologists. Not two generations after this region was cut clean, the spruce have come back. They are a foot thick already, big enough for a latter-day Henry to put under the saw. They will never be cut, however, for most of Desolation is included in the Lincoln Woods Scenic Area. Logging is still a big business in the White Mountain National Forest (ten million dollars a year by the time the harvest reaches its ultimate consumers) but no commercial forestry is permitted in the Lincoln Woods. This entire region, nearly 19,000 acres, has been set aside in a kind of atonement for what J.E. Henry did to the Pemi-gewasset Wilderness.

I keep returning to him, as to a sore tooth. I have said that he owned the Lincoln hospital and the millworkers' houses; what I failed to mention was that he made health insurance available for fifty cents a month, that the houses were rented for ten dollars a month, and that each family received a turkey at Christmas—all this in 1893.

J.E. Henry was sixty-one when he came to Lincoln, and he was universally known as "The Old Man." As the story goes, he presided over every payroll with a gun on his hip. The woodcutter presented a brass tag with his number on it, and he received his pay in cash—minus his purchases from the company store and minus the fines he had incurred that month. The Old Man's pistol was to prevent any argument about these deductions.

Once, when one of his cutters was killed in the woods, J.E. Henry is supposed to have snorted: "Worry about your horses, because they make you money." Toward the end of his career he discovered that tourists would pay good money for a chance to ride to the cuttings. So he ran "Blueberry Specials" every summer. A ticket cost fifty cents to begin with, but later went up to seventy-five; and when it did one of the passengers refused to pay the difference. Old Man Henry stopped the train and wouldn't allow it to proceed until he had received the extra quarter.

He retired in 1908, a year after the infamous fire that burned the lowlands between Mt. Lafayette and Mt. Bond. Ernest Russell visited him in 1909 to prepare an article for *Collier's* magazine. This is how the journalist viewed the timber baron: "Somewhat apart from the closely-clustered village, in a little white-painted house which over-

looks the valley and faces the huge rampart of Loon [Mountain],
lives—if you can call it that—Jim Henry. Sightless, feeble with his
eighty years, relinquishing to his sons, because he must, an industry
that has been the very core of his existence, he frets away his few remaining years."

When he died in 1912, J.E. Henry left a personal estate of about ten
thousand dollars. Of course that did not include his business fortune,
which he had turned over to his sons, and which eventually became
the foundation for the Morgan Memorial in Boston. So when you
patronize the Goodwill Industries, you are joining a philanthropy
that had its beginnings right here in the Pemigewasset Wilderness.

Being wet is a state of mind

Desolation Shelter was the first unsupervised campsite I'd visited since Eliza Brook. It consisted of a lean-to, an outhouse, and a tent platform, with plenty of evidence that tents were commonly erected in the spaces between them. The area was neat enough, but it had a distinctly worn-out appearance—a persuasive argument for the AMC's policy of installing caretakers at heavily used campsites. Playing the role of Frank Vitale or Carol Varner, I decided to put things to right. This was some of the "destination trash" at the shelter: a pair of corduroy hiking shorts, maroon in color; a very soiled undershirt; a pair of flowered panties, pink and lavender; and a recently opened can of Campbell's Baked Beans.

I had no campfire permit, having intended to build no fires. But I figured I'd be doing the Forest Service a favor by breaking the rules on this occasion. I collected scraps of birch bark and other tinder; I built a fire and fed the garments and garbage to it, producing an evil gray smoke that hung around for the better part of an hour. Meanwhile I went swimming in Carrigain Brook, a tributary of the East Branch. There was a splendid view of Mt. Carrigain in the upstream direction, and downstream there were pools enough to refresh a dozen weary hikers.*

When I returned to the lean-to, the afternoon shift was already coming in. They kept coming all afternoon and into the evening, though most of them soon moved out again to tent in the woods. Among the newcomers was a young man with an expedition pack and a haircut like a desert Indian's, long and straight and shorn midway between his earlobes and his shoulders. Since he had no sweatband, he had to keep tossing his head to keep the hair out of his eyes. I enjoyed watching him: he cooked up some kind of pudding soon after his arrival, eating it absently with a soup spoon while he read a paperback copy of *You Can't Go Home Again.* It was twenty years since I'd read a book by Thomas Wolfe, and of course my haircut had been shorter, but his posture reminded me of my own young self. He scraped the pot empty. Then he put Thomas Wolfe face down while he scraped the pot again, with a visual check this time, turning it this way and that while he spooned each last glob of pudding. That done, he cleaned it a third time with his index finger. He was a man who knew how to eat pudding.

I asked him where he was from. "North of New York City," he said, and when I pressed him on that, he said that he lived "near Scarsdale." I gave up. In my experience, nobody from that part of the world will confess his origins, but will say only that he lives *near* Scarsdale; and if he lives in Scarsdale itself he'll say that he comes from Westchester County. I don't pretend to understand this fact, but I offer it as one that my experience has proved.

This lad had been hiking the White Mountains for three weeks now, and he had another week to go. Tomorrow he planned to hike out to the highway and then go down to North Conway for a resupply, staying overnight in the youth hostel there. In case he didn't make it, I gave him a bag of pemmican. I had more than enough to last me through tomorrow, when Sally would meet me with a new batch—this one lighter on the sunflower seeds. In return,

---

**The solution to pollution is dilution. The East Branch flowed
for miles before it served as anyone's drinking water.*

the Scarsdale lad felt obliged to offer me something. He had two Cup-a-Soup packages remaining, split pea and lobster bisque; he offered me the choice. No, I said, you take whichever you want. No, he said, *you* decide. So I took the lobster bisque, and found that it tasted rather like liquid liverwurst.

We talked about campsites. He didn't like the fee system that was in effect at Garfield, Guyot, and the other supervised campsites. Rather than pay a dollar, he pointed out, many campers would pitch their tents in the woods, thereby contributing to the very same wilderness sprawl that the AMC was trying to prevent. I judged that he was talking about himself. I confess to a certain irritation—the grumpiness of middle age, perhaps—but what right had this child of Westchester County to come here with his hundred-dollar pack from Alpine Designs, his ingenious stove from Mountain Research in Seattle, and his goosedown mummy bag from Eddie Bauer or wherever, and with all that expensive gear to expect the AMC to provide him with free lodging?

Still, there was some truth in what he said. There are many backpackers who believe that the "wilderness experience" should be free, no matter how much time and money had been invested to bring the wilderness to the condition in which they are enjoying it. Rather than pay a dollar at a supervised campsite, they will hack out a piece of the wilderness and pitch their tents in it. Aye, and leave their aluminum foil behind them when they move on.

I was too sleepy to argue. By seven o'clock my head was nodding, and I crawled into my own mummy bag, which happens to have been marketed by Sears, Roebuck & Co.

I woke up from time to time, as the three holdovers added new fuel to the fire, or as some new arrival pulled in. One of these was a girl who wanted to know where the toilet was. In my half-awake condition, I was sure that this was the girl whose underwear I had burned (I'd found the panties near the outhouse) and that she had now returned to claim them. The discussion went on for what seemed like a very long time. "That guy in the corner," one of the holdovers said to the girl, as if showing her a particularly interesting feature of Desolation Shelter: "he's been asleep for *three hours.*"

After ten hours I could sleep no more, though I tried. It was a wet Sunday morning—raining at four-thirty, still raining at five, a steady gray drizzle that finally drummed me out of bed. The spruce boughs hung down like green fans, beaded with water. It was all very discouraging.

Desolation Shelter has a three-foot overhang in front, where I could breakfast without disturbing anyone. There was an extra body in the lean-to, beyond the three holdovers and the lad from Scarsdale; and down the trail I could see two blue tents and a red one, magically erected while I had slept. I chewed my pemmican and debated the possibilities. All of them indicated that I should stay where I was: it might stop raining, and even if it didn't, I would be foolish to arrive at the highway before Sally.

At six o'clock one of the tenters strolled down to the river and took a sight at Mt. Carrigain. I asked him where his group was bound. "We'll try for Carrigain," he said, "and if it's too slippery we'll go out to the highway." He was carrying a pot of water with which to cook breakfast. I wondered why he and his friends didn't come down to the lean-to, to cook beneath the overhang, but of course the shelter wasn't their territory. It belonged to those of us who had slept there, and who were now rising one by one, though mostly to return to bed after a yawn, a stretch, and a look at the rain. Only the new man was ambitious enough to start breakfast. His Svea stove was still in the original carton, which made me anxious about the competence of the man who was about to light it. It was just such a stove, I believe, that caused Camp Sixteen Shelter to burn to the ground.

While he fussed with this palmful of Swedish engineering, I asked him where he planned to go this morning. "Out by the shortest route," he said, while flames rolled up yellow and black. When he had the stove going properly, he delved into his pack for pancake flour and a plastic jug of syrup.

I continued my survey, as if a majority vote would cause the rain to stop or to settle in for a day-long drenching, one or the other. Where away? I asked the three holdovers, who were sitting up in their sleeping bags and either reading or staring at the rain. "I'm going to stay right here," said one. "I have an aversion to getting wet." The others felt the same way, even the lad from Scarsdale.

To keep my mind off the pancakes that were now browning in a Boy Scout frypan, I put on my poncho and strolled the neighborhood. Most of the tenters too were staying put. If the rain stopped, they would climb Mt. Carrigain; otherwise they would walk out to the road this afternoon. The mountain was scarcely visible from the viewpoint on the river. Carrigain is a Four Thousand Footer and an exceptionally handsome one; if you draw a circle around the White Mountains, you will find that Carrigain is their central peak. It was not climbed until 1869. So recent is man's acquaintance with the Pemigewasset Wilderness.

On my stroll, I found the metal tip of a cant-hook or peavey, which woodcutters use for rolling logs. Then a section of a two-man cross-cut saw; then a plate from a cast-iron stove. (I could have sworn that it was the same stove that had left another of its pieces at Camp Eighteen.) I carried these relics back to the lean-to and put them on display, as a kind of J.E. Henry Logging Museum.

At nine o'clock I decided to move. I said goodbye to the three hold-overs and to the Scarsdale lad, who was again immersed in Thomas

Wolfe, and I set off on the Carrigain Notch Trail. Soon I hit an old railroad bed where I could swing along between spruce and birch, through Camp Nineteen clearing, and into the woods again. Being wet, I decided, is merely a state of mind. The fear of damp is something that comes with living in a cold climate. Today was warm; therefore I could tolerate a soaking. Seen from this viewpoint the morning was positively beautiful, and I improved it by running through my whole repertoire of Irish ballads—*Jug of Punch, Roddy McCorley, The Rising of the Moon*—learned not at my mother's knee, I am sorry to say, but from records cut by Tommy Makem and the Clancy Brothers.

According to the AMC Guide, I would cross the "infant" East Branch soon after I picked up the Nancy Pond Trail. The infant had grown lusty overnight. It was a small torrent, and the rocks that were supposed to be my stepping-stones were now beneath the surface. But I crossed with the aid of my staff, hopping from stone to stone like a three-legged billygoat.

Soon afterward, the drizzle became a downpour. My boots began to squish and slurp. Ironically, all the minor dips in the trail had recently been bridged with logs, but the major streams had been left to my own ingenuity. The last of these on the ascent was Norcross Brook, where I paused for a final view of the Pemigewasset Wilderness—swirling in mist, green, hilly, and lovely. Then the trail closed in again. It also became a brook in its own right, and I learned not to step on the logs that had been placed there to harden the trail. Some of them were afloat. I bushwhacked wherever I could, moving from one side of the trail to the other as the terrain suggested, and using my walking stick as a fulcrum for the jump. Norcross Pond, when I reached it, was overflowing and pockmarked with rain. Even its lilies were submerged. The bright yellow flowers were still above the water, however, like so many dandelions in a field.

Then the trail became steep and firm as it climbed to the height-of-land, the divide between the Pemigewasset and the Saco. I whooped when I passed over into the Saco watershed. The trail was downhill now, all the way to Crawford Notch. But like the bear that went over the mountain, to see what he could see, I found that this side was pretty much a duplicate of the other. The trail was just as wet, and Nancy Pond too was overflowing its banks. Rivulets crossed the trail at discouragingly frequent intervals. I measured one of these at two feet deep and four feet wide, and I had to cross it downstream on a fallen tree.

Somewhere along here I must have crossed Nancy Brook itself, but I don't remember doing so. Perhaps I mistook it for another wet spot in the trail. Anyhow, the stream was now on my left, pounding and leaping as it rushed down to Crawford Notch, but not visible until suddenly I emerged at the head of Nancy Cascade. On any day this is one of the tallest waterfalls in the White Mountains, dropping several hundred feet to a pool below; today the cascade was a cream-yellow Niagara. When the water met the brink, it was moving so fast that it jetted into the air like the spray from a fire hose, exploding in a halo around any projecting rock, and spume soaked me like a horizontal rain. The roar obliterated every other sound. I stood there for a long time, overwhelmed, and I repeated the tribute when I reached the foot of the cascade. I think that what astonished me most was the color of the froth—not white, as even a dirty stream appears to be white when it breaks over rocks, but *yellow*. Tons of sediment must have moved down Nancy Brook that day.

And the noise, of course. And the wind-blown spray. It was like breasting the Atlantic in the worst nor'easter imaginable.

Let our old friend Starr King explain how Nancy Brook got its name:

"Here, late in the autumn of the year 1778, a poor girl, who lived with a family in Jefferson, was found frozen to death. She was engaged to be married to a man who was employed in the same family where she served. She had entrusted to him all her earnings, and the understanding was, that in a few days they should leave for Portsmouth, to be married there. But . . . the man started with his employer for Portsmouth, without leaving any explanation or message for her. She learned the fact of her desertion on the same day that her lover departed. At once she . . . tied up a small bundle of clothing, and in spite of all the warnings and entreaties, set out on foot to overtake the faithless fugitive. Snow had already fallen; it was nearly night; the distance to the first settlement near the Notch was thirty miles; and there was no road through the wilderness but a hunter's path marked by spotted trees. She pressed on through the night, as the story runs, against a snow-storm and a northwest wind, in the hope of overtaking her lover at the camp in the Notch, before the party should start in the morning. She reached it soon after they had left, and found the ashes of the campfire warm.

"It was plain to those, who, alarmed for her safety, had followed on from Jefferson to overtake her, that she had tried in vain to rekindle the fire in the lonely camp. But the fire in her heart did not falter, and she still moved on, wet, cold, and hungry, with resolution unconquered by the thirty miles' tramp through the wilderness, on the bitter autumn night. She climbed the wild pass of the Notch . . . and followed the track of the Saco towards Conway. Several miles of the roughest part of the way she travelled thus, often fording the river. But her strength was spent by two or three hours of such toil; and she was found by the party in pursuit of her, with her head resting upon her staff, at the foot of an aged tree near 'Nancy's Bridge,' not many hours after she had ceased to breathe. When the

After two days o: rain, Nancy Pond Trail is wet enough to float the logs intended to keep it dry

lover of the unhappy girl heard the story of her faithfulness, her suffering, and her dreadful death, he became insane [and] died, a raving madman. And there are those who believe that often in still nights the valley walls near Mount Crawford echo with the shrieks and groans of the restless ghost of Nancy's lover."

If he was groaning today, I could not hear him for the noise of the water.

There is a kind of picnic ground at the foot of Nancy Cascade, where hikers come up the two miles from the highway to enjoy the waterfall; there are fireplaces assembled from odd bits of stone, and of course the ground is thoroughly beaten down. I could find no sign of the trail through here—it was all trail and a hundred yards wide. I crossed a tributary brook at what seemed a likely spot, but the path I had chosen soon ended in brush and deadfall. I bushwhacked down to the shore of Nancy Brook. There was no trail along the shore, so I bushwhacked to the high ground to the south. It was rough going, steep and brambled; I kept stepping on the skirt of my poncho and snagging it on branches, and snagging also the plastic garbage bag I had used to waterproof my pack. And my glasses fogged over.

There was no trail on the high ground either. I bushwhacked through more brambles and deadfall to the tributary I had just crossed. I crossed it again and made my way back to the picnic ground, where to my joy and relief I found a trail marked with blue scraps of cloth. I followed this new route uphill . . . and emerged at the head of Nancy Cascade, on the very spot where I had been standing an hour before. It was the first time I had ever gone astray in the White Mountains, and on the wettest day. Worst of all I would now be late for my rendezvous with Sally.

I descended again to the picnic ground, resolved that I would sit down and *study* that trail guide, to learn why I kept going wrong. This I did beneath the shelter of the poncho. Meanwhile I smoked a cigarette which I managed to light with one of my emergency matches, a waterproof hoard inside a case that was compass and whistle too.

The description of Nancy Pond Trail is unlike any other in the AMC Guide, which for the most part reads like the instructions that come from the Internal Revenue Service. But whoever wrote the entry for Nancy Pond Trail was very much of an individual. The route was given in such detail that I could have followed it blindfolded, if I was upward bound. Unfortunately I was going in the other direction. Even with a cigarette to soothe me, it was like cracking a safe to reverse the directions. But at last I hit upon the combination: "Near the base of Nancy Cascades, at about 2.2 m. from the start, the trail recrosses to the S. bank." I was on the south bank; I should be on the

north.

This solved part of my problem, but not all. I hadn't thought to cross the stream for the simple reason that the crossing looked impossible. It was not a matter of skipping from stone to stone, because all the stones were submerged.

I rigged myself for the attempt, loosening the pack and leaving its waistband unfastened, so that I could drop it if I fell. Like most things that look difficult, the crossing was easy enough when taken one step at a time. There were stones to walk on, though the water was usually boiling halfway between my ankles and my knees. Only once could I find no stone. I decided to plant my foot on the stream bottom—it wasn't more than two feet deep, after all—but I couldn't do it. Before Vibram could touch gravel, my foot was yanked downstream by the current. So I jumped to the next submerged stone, made it, and then I was across.

In a few hundred yards the trail crossed Nancy Brook again. (I must have come very close to this crossing on my bushwhack.) While I was searching for the best route, I saw two backpackers on the opposite shore, poncho-draped and intent on where they were placing their feet. I couldn't believe that anyone was coming *up* Nancy Pond Trail in a downpour like this one, so I assumed that they had followed me *down,* and had passed me while I was threshing about in the brambles. I yelled at them: where was the best place to cross? They couldn't hear me above the roar of the stream. So I plodded over and caught up with them. They were even more astonished to see me than I had been to see them: a girl and a boy in their early twenties. They stared at me as if I had been one of the rapists in *Deliverance.* No doubt I looked the part, what with a week's growth of beard and the holes in my poncho.

They were heading upstream, after all, and having begun with dry feet they were trying to find a dry place to cross. They said they planned to tent on the shore of Nancy Pond. Remembering the bog that had surrounded it earlier in the day, I suggested that they stop earlier, perhaps in the picnic grove just ahead. In return they told me where to pick up the trail to Crawford Notch.

Then the boy crossed the stream on a fallen tree, oddly holding a packet of food in each hand. Perhaps he was using them for balance. The girl started to follow him, then balked. "I'm not very sure of myself," she said to me. The boyfriend shouted encouragement and instructions from the opposite bank, but of course she couldn't hear him, and couldn't have profited from them anyhow. Advice isn't much use when you are standing on a slippery log and your advisor is safe on the other side. I gave the girl my walking stick. She planted it midway, on a projecting rock, and with this security she crossed over. Then the boyfriend threw the staff back to me, and we waved goodbye.

Nancy Pond Trail had one more surprise for me. Toward the highway the trail had been relocated, jogging off to the right under a series of yellow blazes. I knew perfectly well that if I followed the old trail I would emerge at the place where I'd told Sally to meet me, at the Inn Unique; if I followed the new blazes I would strike the highway some distance to the south. But my confidence had been shaken by that hour in the picnic grounds. So I took the right fork, and of course it put me half a mile below the Inn Unique, and of course Sally wasn't there to greet me.

The first car that went past—*psshssst!* on the wet pavement—froze me like a rabbit. It had been four days since I had seen an automobile and a week since I'd paid any attention to one, and the speed and noise frightened me. I plodded up the highway, and after fifteen weary minutes I spotted the Inn Unique, an English manor house oddly situated at the southern gate of Crawford Notch. Parked on the grass was the little station wagon I called my own.

The innkeeper unique

Crawford Notch is owned in part by the state of New Hampshire, in part by the Morey family. For more than fifty years, Florence Morey has filled the role that was created by the Crawford family—innkeeper, historian, land developer, politician, and tourist attraction. To explain Mrs. Morey is to sketch the history of this remarkable cleft in the mountain. . . .

The earliest settlers in northwestern New Hampshire were obliged to approach it by way of the Connecticut River. As a highway, the river left much to be desired. You traveled upstream at high water and downstream at low, in a log canoe, through rapids that at one point stretched for twenty miles. It was a heroic adventure, not an avenue for commerce, and the North Country could not flourish until an overland route was found.

In 1771 Timothy Nash was hunting moose to the north of Crawford Notch. As the story goes, he climbed a tree to get his bearings and was astonished to see a break in the mountains to the south. He explored the defile, found the Saco River, and followed it down to Conway and the coast, where he reported his discovery to Governor Wentworth in Portsmouth. The governor was pleased but wary. He promised Nash a township if the notch was passable for animals. Nash met this stipulation with the aid of ropes, a fellow hunter, and a long-suffering horse, and the land was duly granted.

Among the first parties to use the new route was that of Colonel Joseph Whipple, who roped his animals through the notch in 1772. He settled in the area now known as Jefferson and became the squire of the North Country. (It was Colonel Whipple's household in which poor Nancy and her faithless lover were employed.) Shortly thereafter, a rough road was built through the notch, crossing the Saco no less than thirty-two times. Jeremy Belknap passed this way in 1784, fresh from a visit with Colonel Whipple. He described the road in his *History of New Hampshire:*

"Along the eastern side of the meadow, under the perpendicular rock, is a causeway of large logs sunk into the mud by rocks, blown with gunpowder from the mountain. On this foundation is constructed a road, which passes through the narrow defile at the south end of the meadow, leaving a passage for the rivulet which glides along the western side. This rivulet is the head of the river Saco. . . . [It] descends toward the south; and at a little distance from the defile its waters are augmented by two streams from the left. . . . Over these are thrown strong bridges; and the whole construction of this road is firm and durable; much labor has been expended upon it, and the net proceeds of a confiscated estate were applied to defray the expense."

By 1792 a pioneer named Abel Crawford was living in a small hut on that meadow to the north. He was joined that year by his father-in-law, Eleazer Rosebrook. Abel felt crowded by his in-laws, so he sold the farm to Eleazer and moved his own family to the south of the notch.

In the eighteenth-century manner, both homes became taverns where the wayfarer could obtain food and lodging. This sideline became a business when the Tenth New Hampshire Turnpike was incorporated in 1803. The turnpike led from Lancaster to Portland by way of the notch, and at last the North Country had a way to send its produce to market. "Well can we remember," wrote Benjamin Willey in his *Incidents in White Mountain History,* "the long trains of Coos teams which used to formerly pass through Conway. In winter, more particularly, we have seen lines of teams half a mile in length; the tough scrubby Canadian horses harnessed to 'pungs,' well loaded down with pork, cheese, butter, and lard." As for the roadside taverns, Willey wrote: "To appreciate fully the necessity there was for these places of shelter, one should pass through the Notch in the depth of winter. The roads are then buried beneath the snow, piled up in drifts to a great depth. This is continually blown about by the wind so as to render impossible a well-beaten path. The traveller has frequently, shovel in hand, to work his way through the mountains."

Ethan Crawford (grandson of Eleazer and son of Abel) inherited the Rosebrook place in 1817. Thus the Crawfords became the squires of the notch. Together they cut the first trail to the summit of Mt. Washington. Between them they hosted almost every personage who visited the White Mountains in those years, from Daniel Webster to Nathaniel Hawthorne. And ultimately they were immortalized in such landmarks as Mt. Crawford, Mt. Tom (for Thomas Crawford), Ethan Pond, the Crawford Path, and of course the notch itself.

Abel's tavern was taken over by his son-in-law, Nathaniel Davis, who in 1846 completed a second bridle path to the summit of Mt. Washington. This route, along the Montalban Ridge, is now known as the Davis Path. It is fifteen miles long and therefore less popular than the Crawford Path; it was even less popular in the 1850s. So all Davis got for his labor was a mortgage on his land. The man who held the mortgage was Samuel Bemis, a wealthy dentist who had retired to "Notchland" in 1840, there to build a stone manor house on the English model. When Davis was unable to make his payments, Dr. Bemis foreclosed on the mortgage. He thus acquired title to a vast tract of wilderness, which in time he bequeathed to his superintendent and man-of-affairs, George Morey by name.

In this century, the Tenth New Hampshire Turnpike has become US 302, and the Bemis house has become the Inn Unique, where latter-day travelers may find food and shelter in a style that has almost been forgotten. From Abel Crawford to his son-in-law—from Nathaniel Davis to his banker—from Samuel Bemis to his superintendent—from George Morey to his daughter-in-law . . . Florence Morey is the fifth in this grand succession, and she wears the mantle well.

The station wagon was locked. I tried all the doors, while a young man in chef's whites watched me from the stone terrace of the inn, no doubt suspecting car theft. To put myself right with the chef, I asked if he knew where the car's driver might be. He didn't. Neither did the woman who greeted me inside the Inn Unique. It was a dark entryway with old portraits in gilt frames, and steel engravings of the White Mountains. "I'll ask . . ." this woman said, and tried a door on the right. "No," she said, retreating from the door. "I think she's asleep." Who was asleep? Sally or Mrs. Morey or somebody else entirely? I felt as if I had fallen through time, as if there was no Sally inside, no car outside, and myself an intruder from another century. Then the door opened again and an older woman appeared—a *grande dame*, in fact. She was not tall by current standards (not nearly so tall as Sally, for example) but she must have been an impressive figure at one time. She wore bifocals with gray plastic frames.

"Has Mrs. Ford registered?" I asked.

"Yes, I'm Mrs. Morey."

"Is Mrs. Ford staying here?" I said, intent on the main idea.

"Ah," said the *grande dame*, extending her hand. "You're Mr. Ford—the lost Mr. Ford!" No doubt I was speaking quietly, inspired by the hush and the gloom and the twelve-foot ceilings of the Inn Unique, but no doubt also that Florence Morey was a bit hard of hearing. Once she understood me, however, she took me briskly in hand. A pretty Nancy was fetched to take me up to room two. All was well; Sally was registered. She had been driving to the trailhead and back for three hours, not knowing whether I would appear there or would take the old route to the inn.

"Do you often have hikers staying here?" I asked Nancy on the stairs.

"When it rains," she said.

Room two was at the upstairs front. It had formerly been Dr. Bemis's library, and as such it was equipped with fireplaces on both the north and south walls. (The house had twelve chimneys when it was built, each with four flues: *forty-eight* fireplaces altogether.) A bathroom had been added in recent years. The carpenters had madly placed the partition so that the south fireplace was divided between the bedroom and the bath. This I observed from the tub, sunk in hot water to my chin, while I quenched the inner flame with a bottle of beer.

Properly clean for the first time in a week, I went with Sally for a tour of Crawford Notch. Sally drove, since I had still not recovered my trust of automobiles. We bought chocolate bars and wooden matches at the Notchland store, just below the state park; and we tried to see the northern entrance as Jeremy Belknap had described it in 1784: "a pass, commonly called the Notch, which in the narrowest part measures but twenty-two feet between two perpendicular rocks." Alas, the highwaymen had changed it. They ran the Saco through a culvert and laid US 302 on top of it, so that the defile became just another narrow place along the highway. The best effects are now to be found to the south, where US 302 clings to a shelf on the mountainside. This stretch of road is especially grand in the winter, when the snowbank has narrowed it to a single lane; or when stormclouds are boiling over the Webster Cliffs, as they were this Sunday afternoon.

We drove back to the Inn Unique for dinner. When Sally turned onto the grass parking lot, the clouds were momentarily torn, and an undeniable patch of blue appeared in the west. The Inn Unique stood in sunshine. It was a manor indeed, a House of Seven Gables, fashioned from granite blocks on the first story and from timbers above that. . . . The granite was quarried some miles away. The rock was drilled at intervals, by hand, and the holes were plugged with wooden dowels: the plugs swelled when wet, splitting the granite as cleanly as if it had been cut with a saw. Oxen dragged these blocks along the Tenth New Hampshire Turnpike, and local men laid them up according to English standards of design. The walls were absolutely true; there was never more than a quarter-inch of mortar between one block and the next.

Florence Morey led us into the dining room, whose ceiling was those embossed metal sheets which I associate with Victorian parlors. "I think I'll seat the Fords here," she said. "This was my grandmother's table. That table beside you came from the Abel Crawford tavern just up the road." We were in front of a window, next to a sideboard with candles as thick as my wrists. Mrs. Morey seated another couple in the opposite corner, also by a window, reminding them that they'd had the same place on their previous visit. The third party tonight was a New York couple and their six-year-old son. The husband was wearing jeans but the wife was in a long dress, which caused Sally to mourn that she hadn't thought to pack something more suited to this gracious room.

Seven guests on a Sunday in July: I began to suspect that the Inn Unique was not a commercial proposition. I had numbered seven employees, counting Mrs. Morey and her son, and I knew that dinner, lodging, and breakfast would cost us less than twelve dollars each. No, the inn was not a business. It was a gentle conspiracy, and we the conspirators. We had been assembled here, staff and guests alike, to support Florence Morey in her role as the last of the White Mountain innkeepers, in a tradition that went back to Abel Crawford himself.

Sally and I took our coffee into the reading room, where after a time Mrs. Morey came to join us. She told us the history of each piece of furniture, some of it belonging to Dr. Bemis and other pieces to her own family, which I understood to be Pendergasts from Massachusetts. (Her aunt, a Pendergast, had served as a nurse in the Civil War, and had seen Lincoln mounted on a horse so small that the president's feet were four inches off the ground.) I followed these stories as best I could, but not always with success. It was nine o'clock, and I had been up since five, had walked nine miles through the rain, and had lost my way besides.

"As you are a hiker," Mrs. Morey said to me, "you must know something about Joe Dodge." I certainly did. Joe Dodge managed Pinkham Notch Camp for most of its existence; he was, in fact, the AMC's North Country division from young manhood until his retirement, and the new residential building at Pinkham was named in his honor. "Oh, that," Mrs. Morey said of the Joe Dodge Center. "I think some architect took the AMC for a ride when he came up with *that* design. It doesn't belong in the mountains. Not the way this building does."

She told us how she had visited Boston with the young Joe Dodge, in the 1920s, in a Model T truck with its side curtains flapping in the breeze. It was the winter following the birth of his first child. Joe had outfitted Pinkham Notch Camp with a dogsled to that he could reach Gorham and a doctor, in case the baby took sick: the Pinkham Notch road was not plowed in those years. As Florence Morey told the story, the AMC "hierarchy" called Joe to account for this innovation:

"Joe, is it true you have a dog team at Pinkham Notch?"

"Yes it is."

"Well, Joe, we want you to understand that the AMC is a *hiking* club, not a *dog* club. You'll have to give up your job or your dogs, one or the other."

On the way home from Boston, Joe decided that he liked the job more than the security of his dog team. He decided to sell, and the AMC in turn bent its principles far enough to allow the Dodge family a single dog. So Joe went out and purchased the largest animal he could find. "I don't know what kind of dog it was," Mrs. Morey concluded with great satisfaction, "but it stretched from the end of this couch to that fireplace over there"—a distance of ten feet.*

Then she told us how Crawford Notch State Park had come into existence, the land seized for twelve dollars an acre, and that despite some irregularities in the engrossing of the bill. "So the state has the upper end of the notch and I have the lower end," she said, "and sometimes we even speak to each other." To judge by the vinegar in her voice, those conversations were not always friendly.

Actually, the state legislature intended to take the southern end of the notch as well. Most of this land, north and south, had belonged to Abel Crawford, from whose callused hands it passed to Nathaniel Davis, Dr. Bemis, and finally the Morey family. The precise acreage is nowhere stated. In his *Chronicles of the White Mountains*, Frederick Kilbourne described it as "a vast tract of woodland, extending for miles up the Notch." Anyhow, by 1911 there was a great movement to secure the White Mountains from private exploitation. People

---

It was a malamute named Hui-Skookum. Apparently the AMC "hierarchy" came to accept Joe's dog, for when the animal died in 1938 it was given an obituary in Appalachia.

were beginning to tour the North Country in their automobiles, and they understood for the first time what a treasure New Hampshire possessed. Thus 1911 was the year of the Weeks Act, by which Congress indirectly established the White Mountain National Forest. It was also the year in which the state of New Hampshire decided to take Crawford Notch out of private hands.

As Mrs. Morey said, the bill authorizing the purchase was defective. Among other things, the legislators forgot to provide for a bond issue. The attorney general ruled that the governor could make the purchase anyhow, but that he couldn't buy any more land than he could afford from the current operating budget. At twelve dollars an acre, this turned out to be six thousand acres, which is the present extent of Crawford Notch State Park.

Well, twelve dollars was a week's wages for most people in 1911, and the transaction must have involved $72,000, so it cannot be described as highway robbery. Nevertheless, it was still a source of great annoyance to Mrs. Morey.

Nor am I sure which would have proved to be the better custodian of Crawford Notch, the Morey family or the New Hampshire Division of Parks. The Moreys of course are in the real estate business. ("A few acres sometimes we sell," according to the brochure for the Inn Unique; "private use only.") The state, on the other hand, has given us a campground, a souvenir shop and lunch counter, parking lots, an arts-and-crafts store, and—until very recently—a menagerie of native wildlife.

Pack animals zero xiii

On Monday the clouds were bellying through Crawford Notch, dropping showers at unpredictable intervals. So, like the ranging companies of old, I "lay still by reason of rain." (I am thinking of Capt. Samuel Willard's journey to the mountains in 1725. The rangers met no Indians, but traveled prodigious distances if their estimates are to be believed; they passed through the Pemigewasset Wilderness until they struck the "headwaters of Saco," perhaps right here at the southern gate of Crawford Notch.) I improved the day by telephoning the reservations secretary at Pinkham Notch Camp. She said that Lakes of the Clouds Hut was booked full on Wednesday, but that she could offer me a backpacker space on Thursday. "No meals," she explained. "There's a room set aside where you can cook."

"All right," I said. "What about Pinkham Notch Camp on Friday?"

"Yes."

"What about Carter Notch on Saturday?"

"Just barely," she told me. "I have one space left."

Ah wilderness! With my reservations secure, I now required a hiking permit for the Davis Path. The permit, I was told, could be obtained at the state park headquarters in Crawford Notch. The office was closed when we arrived, but I was sent around to a cabin in the woods, where I found a young man and a cat named Sam. They opened the office for me, Sam riding on the young man's shoulder.

The permit was Form No. 2300-30. It called for my name and address, the name of the wilderness area I was visiting, the inclusive dates, point of entry and point of exit, primary method of travel, number of people in my party, number of pack animals, and number of watercraft. Then I signed my name beneath this pledge: *I agree to abide by all laws, rules, and regulations which apply to this area.* The signature was witnessed by Sam's owner, who tore off the top copy for me and kept a carbon for the Forest Service computers.

"Carry it with you," he advised. "They enforce it."

I folded the permit and put it into my pack. At some future time I would emerge as a statistic: resident of New Hampshire, traveling alone, with zero pack animals and zero watercraft, spent three days of July in the Presidential-Dry River Wilderness. . . .

A wilderness, as defined by Congress, is "an area where the earth and its community of life are untrammeled by man, where man himself is a visitor who does not remain." That is a lovely definition, and one that is broad enough to include any part of the White Mountains except a few ski areas, campgrounds, and tourist concessions. The Forest Service has a different interpretation, believing that the Wilderness Act of 1964 can apply only to land that has *never* been trammeled. That excludes just about every acre this side of the Mississippi. Of the fifty-four wilderness areas approved in the first ten years, only two were in the east and only one was in New England, that one being the Great Gulf Wilderness north of Mt. Washington. And it was only 5,500 acres, just barely qualifying under the law.

Since it was clear that the Forest Service was more interested in timber production than in "earth and its community of life," Congress took matters back into its own hands. In 1975 a new bill was drafted: "Congress finds and declares that it is in the national interest that . . . areas in the eastern half of the United States be promptly designated as wilderness within the National Wilderness Preservation System." In the White Mountain National Forest, four new tracts were proposed, totaling 83,000 acres. The opposition was fierce, especially from the loggers and the snowmobilers who would thus be excluded from more than ten percent of the national forest. In the end, two of the proposed areas were dropped, and parts of the other two were joined together as the Presidential-Dry River Wilderness, 20,000 acres between US 302 and timberline on Mt. Washington.

The Davis Path runs up the middle of this tract, along the high ground known as the Montalban Ridge.

With my reservations and my permit, then, I set off for the wilderness on Tuesday morning. (I also had a new supply of pemmican, and a new poncho to replace the one I had torn on Sunday.) No doubt I should have walked the quarter-mile from the Inn Unique to the trailhead, but the car was available and the hour was late, so I accepted Sally's offer of a ride. The highway had recently been improved along here. As a result, the trailhead was marooned behind guard rails and a high embankment; we had to park beyond it and walk back. The Saco roared below, still busy with Sunday's runoff. I don't understand how canoes and kayaks can navigate the rivers of the White Mountains. Even at high water they are strewn with boulders as big as automobiles.

The Saco was spanned by one of the AMC's fabulous suspension bridges, fifty feet long and two feet wide between the handrails. It jumped wildly with every step. Altogether it reminded me of one of those vine bridges over a South American gorge—something out of the adventure stories of my youth—though the cables in this case were made of steel. The uprights were fastened to the floorboards with hinges, the better to flex as we crossed over. Sally didn't like it much. She returned to the other shore with all the concentration of a passenger being rescued from a sinking ship, and it wasn't until she was safely across that she turned to wave. Goodbye again, Sally. I love you, the more so because if you object to these excursions of mine, you keep remarkably quiet about it. . . . What I didn't know was that she would drive the long way home, through Plymouth, where she would buy a brass bed of uncertain age but undeniable beauty: it would be set up when I returned the following Monday, on our wedding anniversary. Sally keeps me on a long leash but a strong one.

The trail now divided, left, right, and straight ahead. They all seemed equally acceptable, so my first act on the Davis Path was to drop my pack and get out the AMC Guide. "Beyond the E end of the bridge," it directed me, "continue E across an overgrown field to the edge of the woods and turn SE." I chose the right fork as being southeasterly. It took me in short order to someone's backyard, with laundry on the clothesline and a dog growling nearby, but it was the Davis Path without doubt, for a white arrow on a brown background pointed me into the trees. This was as it should have been: "At about ¼ m., the path turns E, enters the woods (sign), crosses a dry brook and . . . soon enters the old, carefully graded bridle path." The brook was not dry this morning, but it was narrow enough for me to jump across. I found myself on the bridle path—compacted earth with scarcely any sign of erosion, neatly switching back and forth as it climbed to the high ground.

I was soon in a sweat. Even a one-day layover had been enough for me to revert to a sidewalk rush, my four-mile-an-hour lowland stride. Or perhaps it was the mosquitoes that spurred me on. Anyhow I was overheating my engine, so I stopped for water, salt tablets, and an application of bug repellent. Then I returned to the attack, climbing two thousand feet in the first two miles, and at eleven o'clock I was on the ridge, on a granite ledge above the notch. The highway ran to the south, strangely empty of traffic. Below me and to the west was the Inn Unique, a toy building beside the road, and behind it was the fold in the mountains through which I had come on Sunday in the rain; and behind that was the stupendous profile of Mt. Carrigain. I was astonished at its majesty, because from most viewpoints Carrigain is handsome but not impressive.

I was also surprised by the height-of-land between the Pemi and the Saco, over which I had marched the day before yesterday. Seen from here it was a mighty obstacle. Nor was I mistaken about the route, because I could clearly see the white flash of Nancy Cascade, both the upper and lower falls, where I had stood in the roar and blown spray on Sunday afternoon. If you want to marvel at what you have accomplished, find a high spot and look at the mountains themselves; if you want to minimize the difficulties ahead, study the map.

From Mt. Crawford to Mt. Resolution, the Davis Path almost exactly follows the 3,000-foot contour line. Nathaniel Davis was not interested in any summit but the one that towered to the north, so he slabbed the ridge whenever he could, keeping to the level grade. He cut this first four miles in a single summer, 1844, no doubt with strong sons to help him, but still it was a herculean task. Anyone who doubts the hardship should leave the trail for a time and try to force a path through the tangled scrub that grows on a ridgeline such as this. Cutting a trail is backbreaking labor. Locating where the trail should go, in such terrain, does not break the back so much as it breaks the heart.

Along the way I met two young men who had tented overnight at Resolution Shelter. "It was full," they told me. "There were eight Girl Scouts when we arrived, and they wouldn't let us in, but we found a place to pitch our tent."

"How far?" I asked.

"Oh, you're almost there."

I thought they meant a mile or two, since hikers are loath to discourage one another, but in fact they were telling the truth. It was twelve o'clock exactly when I reached the junction. The lean-to was down a steep side-trail to the left; Mt. Resolution was on the Parker Trail to the right; and the Davis Path went straight ahead. I could have pushed on to Isolation Shelter and reached it in time for supper. But that would put me a day ahead of schedule at the AMC hostels, and furthermore there was the problem of the Girl Scouts. I hadn't met them on the trail, so they must have been heading north. If they spent the night at Isolation Shelter, I might be obliged to sleep in my polyethylene tube, and that was an experience I wanted to avoid if possible. So I turned left.

It was the steepest scramble of the day, down to a shelf of land not quite large enough to contain the lean-to that had been built there nearly fifty years ago. I knew the shelter when I saw it: facing a blackened ledge, the best place imaginable to spend a chilly evening. The open front was about six feet from the ledge, where a fireplace had been mortared in place, perfectly situated to throw its heat into the shelter. With a good fire burning, Resolution Shelter would serve as a reflector oven. That was the case in 1964, when I had stayed here with the lawyer and the realtor. We represented the old school of mountain walking—grown men on a weekend lark, in the bough-bed and campfire days. We'd roasted ourselves in front of that fireplace one chilly evening, drinking whiskey from small bottles which we had independently secreted in our rucksacks. It was like the miracle of the loaves and fishes when we began to produce those bottles.

As it happened, I was off the cigarettes that fall. But a lone hiker came in after sundown, and he was a smoker. I was in torment. A campfire, tired muscles, a cup of whiskey and Tang—and beside me this friendly stranger with a firefly glow at his lips. Finally I could bear it no longer, and I swapped my last little jug for a cigarette.

Now I lunched alone on pemmican. Drying off in the sun, I felt chilly, so I put on a shirt and set off to climb Mt. Resolution. The mountain was named in tribute to Nathaniel Davis: he pushed his bridle path this far in 1844, then despaired, but started anew the following year. That was resolution indeed.

The summit is about half a mile from the Davis Path, and its altitude is a mere thirty-five hundred feet, so naturally we ignored it in 1964. The same was true of all the peaks along the Montalban Ridge—Crawford, Stairs, and Davis—except for Mt. Isolation, which stood five feet above the magic Four Thousand mark. Now I would redeem myself, enjoying the views I had missed in the rush to bag Mt. Isolation.

I heard voices while I followed the obscure trail to the summit, over ledges where blueberry bushes grew in every crack. Two men were resting at a large cairn near the top. They had taken off their boots and socks and were letting them dry in the sun. I said hello. The larger and older man (they were brothers, as it turned out) stared at my shirt pocket. "Do you have *cigarettes*?" he said. "My God, I've been wanting a cigarette ever since I woke up this morning." I gave him one, and also a light, and told him how history was repeating itself on Montalban Ridge. Meanwhile a third man came into view from the south. He was carrying a rucksack, the first I'd seen on this trip, and he was suffering both from the drag on his shoulders and from blisters on his feet.

The rucksack made me feel nostalgic. I thought perhaps he was a throwback to the old days, but he wasn't. "I bought it because it was cheap," he said, "and now I'm sorry."

They'd spent last night at Langdon Shelter to the south; they had reservations at Lakes of the Clouds Hut for tonight, but it was obvious that they couldn't make it. Mt. Washington was an impossible distance to the north. It was in and out of the clouds; when the summit was clear we could see the television and radio masts, like minarets against the sky. It looked just like the Enchanted Castle that introduces the Disney show on Sunday evenings—a mountaintop, a jumble of buttresses and keeps, and the spires reaching up to no apparent purpose. Below it was the great scarred face of Oakes Gulf, the southernmost and largest of the ravines scooped out of Mt. Washington by the retreating glaciers.

Between us and the summit there were the undistinguished humps of the Montalban Ridge, which I would be hiking Wednesday and Thursday. West of them were the Southern Presidentials, which were probably mobbed with hikers this afternoon in July, for along that ridge lay Monroe, Eisenhower, Clinton, and Jackson—Four Thousand Footers all—not to mention an AMC hostel, the Appalachian Trail, and the shortest route to Mt. Washington from the south.

On a northwest line from where we stood, we could look into Crawford Notch, its eastern wall formed by the Webster Cliffs, its western wall by Willey, Field, and Avalon. Due west were Mt. Guyot and the Bonds, and beyond them a blue haystack that was probably Mt. Lafayette, which I had climbed five days ago. South and west was the same vista I had seen from the Crawford ledges, including Carrigain's great bulk and the glint of Nancy Cascade.

The three hikers decided to drop down to Resolution Shelter for lunch. I explored the summit of Mt. Resolution, a queer place of ledge, dead trees, dwarf fir, blueberry bushes, and lichen that grew in fantastic clumps. These clumps were the size of apples; they made me think of how the vegetation might look on Venus or Mars. I wished I knew more about the things that grow in the earth. But I didn't, so I contented myself with hunting blueberries across the summit ledges, getting in all a scant handful. A week later and I would have had a feast.

The three hikers were still at Resolution Shelter when I came down from the summit. We introduced ourselves. They had decided to forego their reservations at Lakes of the Clouds and sleep instead at Isolation Shelter. "Seven miles," said Gregg, the older of the brothers and the man who'd bummed the cigarette from me. "We ought to make it in three hours." I thought that this was an optimistic assessment, and so did the man with the rucksack, for he groaned and said that he would start forthwith, that the brothers could catch up with him on the trail. They were lunching on pepperoni, cheese, and pilot biscuits. Gregg offered me some. I declined, of course, but I took a chunk of pepperoni the second time it was offered. That squared us for the cigarette, so when they were packing up Gregg asked me for another. My return this time was a fruit bar and the last of the pilot biscuits.

They were the last people I saw that day. Toward four o'clock I heard hallooing on the trail, but it must have been joy at the milestone passed, since nobody came down the side-path to join me. I amused myself by reading the graffiti on the inside walls of the lean-to. It was as artistic as any I have seen in the mountains. There was a graphic representation of *Clover,* which I took to be somebody's name, with trefoils sprouting between the letters; there was also a tribute to a rock group, the Grateful Dead. These were recent additions, as was one that boasted: "What a great place to expand one's mind!"

The older signatures went back to 1931, names and dates penciled upon the wood. Some of these were repeats. Russell Kueling and Stanford Davis were here on July 8, 1940, and again on August 4, 1946. The dates were evocative. What had Kueling and Davis done in the six years between their visits to Resolution Shelter? Gone to war, perhaps.

I was not the only visitor to ponder those faded pencil marks. Loreen Hurley had studied them too, and added this: "Did the people who wrote here in the 1930s expect us to read what they wrote in the 1970s? I don't expect the people in the year 2010 to read *this.*" She concluded on a gloomy note: "There might not be mountains." Oh yes, Loreen, the mountains will be here, though Resolution Shelter may long since be gone, and your wonder with it.

The black flies on the Montalban Ridge were stupid creatures. They didn't know that black flies are supposed to disappear when the air turns chilly. I put on a sweater and climbed onto the roof of the lean-to, to catch the last warmth of the sun; the black flies accompanied me. Through the birch leaves overhead I watched the sky—now cumulus, now mares' tails scudding south from Stairs

Mountain, and now a mackerel sky. In half an hour I exhausted my knowledge of the clouds. Except for the thunderheads, I'd seen every kind of sky I knew, and what did that portend for tomorrow's weather? Variable conditions, no doubt. Then the sky was blue again, with occasional white puffballs of cumulus. When I was very small, I used to lie on an abandoned jetty on Lake Winnipesaukee and watch the clouds go by, until it seemed that they were stationary, that it was I who was in motion. . . . Overhead, a darning needle was swooping. What did darning needles eat—black flies? Then why didn't he swoop down and enjoy the insects that were enjoying me? The sun moved behind the Webster Cliffs—into Crawford Notch as it seemed to me—and the trees on Stairs Mountain turned gray with dusk. A while ago I'd heard a diesel locomotive groaning along the Maine Central tracks, past Bemis Station to the height-of-land, but now there was no sound but the brook below me and the leaves above. It occurred to me that in all likelihood no human being would sleep within four miles of me tonight. This was solitude, as such things are measured in the Northeast; this was the hiker's dream. . . . No, that couldn't be the case, because in more than a week I'd met only two hikers who were traveling alone. But I was solitary, and I was drunk on it.

Was my mind expanding? No doubt, no doubt.

I jumped down from my perch and cleared the charred logs from the fireplace, billets two feet long and six inches thick; I stacked them under cover in the shelter, for the enjoyment of the next troop of Girl Scouts. As for myself, I had learned how to build fires in Vietnam. (That too was in 1964. I was a reporter, not a soldier, though people kept sticking weapons into my hand. The war was very informal in those days.) The Vietnamese soldiers were thrifty with their fires, as they were obliged to be thrifty with everything else. They would gather three or four rocks the size of an Oriental fist, arranging them in a circle small enough to support a cookpot, and in this confined space they would build a fire of twigs, feeding it constantly until the rice water came to a boil. All of which took no more than fifteen minutes. Whereas a campfire of Girl Scout dimensions requires an hour to build and twice that long to burn itself out. I had struck a compromise between East and West: no firewood bigger than my thumb.

Even at that, my campfire outlasted the dusk, and I found my sleeping bag with the aid of my flashlight. I placed my boots beside my head. Into one boot went my glasses; into the other went the flashlight and the insect repellent, and to sleep.

But oddly enough it was a restless night. The resident mouse was interested in my pack, and he kept startling me awake. There had been mice—or chipmunks, squirrels, or raccoons—at every other lean-to along the route, but they had never troubled my sleep. It is a queer thing, but true: night noises are fearsome when you are alone, while the presence of total strangers on the same bed of boards will guarantee an unbroken sleep.

Pack
Animals
Zero

You can't satisfy everyone

At six-thirty I breakfasted on Stairs Mountain, whose dramatic steps I had seen yesterday through the trees. Beneath my heels was the top-most riser—what appeared to be a hundred-foot drop. There was a second step beneath that one, but like the ledges which form the Old Man of the Mountains, the Giant Stairs are not in line with each other, so I couldn't make it out from the summit.

The view was a 180-degree sweep from east to west, very like the one I had enjoyed from the Crawford ledges yesterday morning. To the

south, though, I could now see a patch of silver that was probably
Conway Lake; my map did not reach that far, so I couldn't be sure.
And of course the Montalban Ridge was lengthening behind me, Mt.
Crawford and Mt. Resolution now added to the foreground, as if I
were a spider on the face of the earth, spinning summits as I moved
along.

Meanwhile the sun was climbing to my left, throwing the great
shadow of Stairs Mountain upon the western wall of Crawford
Notch. I stood up and waved my arms, expecting to see a shadow-
man return the wave from Mt. Bemis. It didn't happen. As the sun
rose above the trees behind me, the silhouette of Stairs Mountain
plunged deeper into the notch, and my image if any was lost in the
forest below.

Nearby, on the true summit, I found a strip of white cloth about
twenty feet long and three feet wide, pegged down by billets of wood.
It could have served no other purpose than to identify Stairs Mountain from above. I was tempted to write a message on the cloth. A
satellite might pass overhead today, silent in the vacuum of space, its
long-range cameras dumbly clicking; my message might be relayed
to a ground station somewhere, sent to Washington, and read by a
technician in the employ of the U.S. Geological Survey:
halloooooo. . . . It would pep up his day, certainly. It might even
make him yearn for the days when he would have measured Stairs
Mountain by carrying a barometer to the summit, measuring the
drop in atmospheric pressure, and judging thereby its altitude above
the sea. Compared to satellite photography, the barometer was a
primitive instrument. But it must have been a whole lot more re-
warding for the man who took the measurements.

I moved on. The Davis Path, from Mt. Resolution onward, no
longer followed the 3,000-foot contour. Instead I was continually
dipping into cols—all of them marshy—and climbing up again. The
cols were a lesson in how trails are walked to death. As the vegetation
died beneath the hiking boots, the soil lost its stability and turned to
mud. Then I came along and sought the dry ground to either side—
helping kill more plants in my turn. The end of this process is a
wallow of such dimensions that it no longer makes sense to walk
around it. Then the trail crews go to work, bridging the mire with
logs split down the middle. That solves the immediate problem while
posing another, for now the trail is passable for hikers who insist on
keeping their feet dry.

In the case of the Davis Path, this process will be hastened by the
wilderness label recently attached to it. (Like the "scenic vista" signs
along New Hampshire highways: the label doesn't change the vista
in the slightest, but it certainly increases the number of tourists who
stop to admire it.) At Desolation Shelter, four nights ago, I'd mentioned the Montalban Ridge to the lad who lived near Scarsdale. "I

haven't been over there," he told me. "But I keep meeting people who
tell me it's a very nice place to be, and that they plan to go over there
the next chance they get." This was said in the manner of a fisherman sharing knowledge of his favorite stream, except that these
fishers of wilderness had not yet cast their lines on the Montalban
Ridge, but had only heard of it at second hand. And was it the ridge
that attracted them, or the wilderness label newly attached to it?

So the traffic will increase, and likewise the improvements, until
the Davis Path resembles those marvelously engineered portions of
the Kinsman Ridge Trail upon which I began this hike. A kind of
I-93 for backpackers. Perhaps something like this was in Loreen
Hurley's mind when she worried about what the year 2010 would
bring. *There might not be mountains,* meaning that the mountains
won't be like the ones we have known: the ragged peaks and the
lonely shelters, and muddy boots wherever the trail dips into a col.

Nathaniel Davis bypassed the summit that was later named for
him. So had I on my previous visit. Now I scrambled up the side-trail
to Mt. Davis and found it to be a flat place of ledge and scrub and
blueberry bushes, warm in the nine o'clock sun. I decided to take off
my boots and stay a while.

The weather was gloomy in the west, over the Southern Presidentials. Clouds were sheeting across Eisenhower's noble skull. Seen
from this angle, the great bald dome bore an uncanny resemblance to
that of the late president, for whom it was named in 1969. (Renamed,
I should say. The original title was Mt. Pleasant, which struck me as
infinitely less suitable.) Hard by that rocky summit was Mt.
Clinton—another peak caught up in the nomenclature game. The
New Hampshire legislature passed a bill in 1913 to rename Clinton
"in honor of Franklin Pierce, fourteenth president of the United
States, and the only citizen or resident of New Hampshire who has
been the incumbent of that exalted office." Nobody paid the slightest
attention to the change.

To the north, Mt. Washington was smothered in a cloud of its own.
The cloud was forming just beyond Mt. Monroe and was pouring
eastward along the "large level or plain of a day's journey over," of
which John Josselyn had written; it topped off at Boott Spur on the
east, at an elevation of 5,500 feet. Mt. Washington makes its own
weather, as New Hampshiremen like to say. Moist air comes in from
the west and climbs the mountain, cooling as it climbs, so that the
moisture condenses into a cloud. If the air is wet enough, part of the
burden must be dropped in the form of rain or snow. So Mt. Washington is often storm-bound even in fair weather, let alone a variable
day like this one.

After an hour on the ledges, with the warm sun and the cool breeze
working pleasantly on me, I set out again on the Davis Path. In

another mile I reached the side-trail to Mt. Isolation. As I climbed it, I heard voices above me. They belonged to a middle-aged couple who were bagging the Four Thousand Footers; they'd come over Monroe and Eisenhower yesterday, had dropped down to Dry River Shelter last night, and would trek back to Lakes of the Clouds Hut this afternoon. They were awed by the prospect. It did indeed seem a mighty haul, up to Boott Spur and westward at cloud level, to the hut tucked somewhere below the modest summit of Mt. Monroe. In truth the distance was less than five miles.

After they left, I explored the summit of Isolation, finding new evidence of the U.S. Geological Survey at play. The summit was marked by a tremendous *Y*, fifty feet long as I paced it off. The cloth had been here for some little time, to judge by the number of waffle-stomper soles that had marched across it.

Due west of Isolation is the AMC hostel at Mizpah Spring. Eleven years earlier I stood on this same mountain, watching that hut under construction and damning the AMC for putting it there. With bunk-rooms, flush toilets, and a crew-served kitchen, it replaced a perfectly lovely shelter of the lean-to type. The hut cost $115,000 and filled what the AMC regarded as a "gap" in its chain of hostels, between Lakes to the north and Zealand to the south. A few tent platforms were added later, in an effort to provide for hikers who couldn't afford the tariff at the hut, but of course it wasn't the same. The tenters felt like poor relations at the feast, welcome to step inside for a look but not to sit down for dinner. And the paying guests felt jostled by the tenters, especially on a stormy evening when there might be a hundred people in the common room. "It's too bad those platforms are there," a hut-goer once told me, rather overlooking the fact that it was the hostel that intruded upon the backpackers' domain, not the other way around.

You can't satisfy everyone. Maybe, after a certain point, you can't satisfy anyone.

Two peak-baggers on the summit of Isolation. Three more on the Davis Path—a girl and two boys, upward bound—and at the shelter a fisherman and his two young sons just arriving from the east. Despite its name, Isolation was the busiest junction on the Montalban Ridge.

The fishermen came from North Carolina. They'd slept at Rocky Branch Shelter last night, and after lunch they intended to climb Mt. Washington. "We have taller mountains down home," one of the boys assured me. I told him that in New Hampshire we preferred not to talk about Mt. Mitchell or Clingmans Dome, and that in any event Mt. Washington was a special place, as he would soon discover. He shrugged. "The fish are bigger, too," he said, "and besides that we have *snakes*." Which caused me to notice that the North Carolinians were wearing boots that reached halfway to their knees.

The boys were desperate to build a campfire, but their father insisted on canned alcohol. He had a little Sterno stove in his pack and he set it up beside the fireplace. It didn't work very well, because the breeze cooled the soup almost as fast as the alcohol flame could heat it. They were two hours altogether on their lunch break. Then they set off for Mt. Washington, not entirely sure what they would do when they reached it. They'd left their car near the village of Glen, twenty-four miles to the south as the highway ran.

Meanwhile I looked for the water supply that had been promised in the AMC Guide. It proved to be a murky trickle to the eastward, downstream from the shelter, the trail, and the latrine. I used my plastic cup as a dipper, an ounce here and an ounce there, working upstream to avoid the mud I was stirring from the bottom. When the canteen was reasonably full, I added five Halazone tablets; and I waited half an hour before using the stuff for so much as brushing my teeth. I was very glad that I would have no dishes to wash in that stream.

Two more hikers came in that afternoon. The first was an unemployed construction worker from Nashua who had begun his peak-bagging career on Saturday, and who had climbed twelve mountains in the past five days. He was vague about his immediate plans. He might climb Isolation, or then again he might not; he might drop down to Dry River Shelter and go over the Southern Presidentials tomorrow, or he might spend the night right here. "I'm running out of ambition," he confessed. "How far to Isolation?" I told him that he could go to the summit and back in fifteen minutes if he left his pack at the shelter, and that since he'd come this far he might as well bag it. So he set off. While he was gone, I hefted his pack and discovered why his ambition was running out. I could barely lift it from the ground. It weighed sixty-five pounds, as the Nashuan admitted when he returned from bagging Isolation. He didn't like to cook, so he carried canned food exclusively; he needed a lot of fluid, so he carried a five-quart army water bag; and he was afraid of losing his way, so he carried a revolver. Wouldn't a whistle have been more convenient? "Yes," he said, "but you can't hear a whistle very far. But three shots—anybody can hear that, and it's bound to attract attention."

I'm not sure what else he carried, to make up that tremendous burden, but I did notice that he kept his matches in a glass jar. He had a tent as well, though he'd never used it, and a weighty sleeping bag like those used by roadside campers.

The second arrival, by contrast, might have served to illustrate a backpacker's catalog. Everything he carried was the best and the lightest. He was very severe and straight in his bearing, yet he wore shoulder-length hair and a T-shirt emblazoned with a tribute (the second I'd seen in two days) to the Grateful Dead. Altogether, he reminded me of a young schoolmaster who for reasons of his own had disguised himself as one of the flower children, using television images as his model. I asked him if he had ever been to Resolution Shelter, to add to the graffiti there, but it seemed that this was his first visit to the Montalban Ridge—and that by accident. He'd intended to camp in the Great Gulf Wilderness on the other side of Mt. Washington. All the overnight permits had been spoken for, however, so he'd signed up for Thursday night and was stopping here betimes.

This was fascinating stuff to the Nashuan, who had never heard of the wilderness system and who had no permit to be on the Montalban Ridge. "What do they do if they catch you without one?" he asked.

I didn't know, and neither did the young man who admired the Grateful Dead. It seemed unlikely that a forest ranger would visit Isolation Shelter at nightfall or that, if he did, he would do anything more than write out a permit on the spot. Like the income tax, the permit system must depend on willing compliance rather than stern enforcement.

Then the North Carolinians came down the trail. They'd reached the first outlook northward, saw that they'd never reach the summit this afternoon, and so were returning to their lean-to on the Rocky Branch. They soon left us, but not before the boys made another attempt to start a campfire. It smouldered for some little time, doing nothing to reduce the black-fly population. The bugs swarmed about the Nashuan and me, but the Grateful Dead seemed immune to them. He spent the rest of the afternoon sitting on a rock and writing in a blue spiral-bound notebook.

The Nashuan had canned stew for dinner, followed by canned peaches. The Grateful Dead brought out a trail stove and worked up a meal of freeze-dried something or other. I ate my pemmican. I was growing weary of pemmican by this time, although Sally's mixture (brought to me at Crawford Notch) was better than mine. She hadn't ground it so fine, and I could vary the meal by such stratagems as leaving the apricots for dessert. She'd reduced the volume of sunflower seeds, too, as I had urgently requested by telephone from Lafayette Campground.

STOP

THE AREA AHEAD HAS THE WORST WEATHER IN AMERICA.
MANY HAVE DIED THERE FROM EXPOSURE, EVEN IN THE
SUMMER. TURN BACK NOW IF THE WEATHER IS BAD.

WHITE MOUNTAIN NATIONAL FOREST

The enchanted castle   xv

Since he would have company in that direction, the Nashuan decided to walk back toward Mt. Washington next morning. His latest plan was to make a U-turn on the Crawford Path, hike the Southern Presidentials, and tent overnight at Mizpah Spring Hut. Or else he would splurge on meals and a bunk. Or else he would push on to the highway by the shortest route. "I have a feeling," he confessed, "that this trip is coming to an end." Meanwhile I was packing my gear, which puzzled the Nashuan. "Don't you even eat breakfast?" he asked.

"On the trail," I said. "I'll wait for you at treeline."

He was afraid to walk alone above treeline—a sensible fear, and one that seemed to play a very large role in determining his route on any given day.

It was a fine, steady climb to the unnamed summit where the North Carolinians had turned back. I was there by six o'clock. I found a nest of tree roots and settled down to eat breakfast and to admire the Enchanted Castle atop Mt. Washington. The summit was clear this morning. Otherwise the weather was the same as yesterday's, with gray clouds sheeting in from the west and breaking up as they passed overhead. Briefly, the sun touched the Enchanted Castle. Then the summit dropped back into shadow. I was looking into the great scarred face of Oakes Gulf, its headwall slicing the cone of Mt. Washington and making it look smaller than it actually was; to the right was the sharp point of Boott Spur, and beneath that a rounded hump that seemed to be at treeline. I would walk across that hump, across Boott Spur, and across the almost level plain beyond; then I would ascend the cone to the Enchanted Castle. It is rare that we have our morning's work laid out for us with such clarity.

By my reckoning, Darby Field saw this identical view when he came to Mt. Washington in 1642, the first man of European blood to make the ascent.

There is no shortage of Indian legends about this summit. We are told, for example, that the Great Spirit dwelled among the clouds on Mt. Washington, so that mortals ventured here on pain of death. We are also told (in what strikes me as a contradiction) that this peak was the Ararat for an Indian Noah and his wife, who repeopled the world after a great flood. Unfortunately these legends were reported by white men, not by the native Americans. They may contain some echo of the Indian story-teller, making myth around the campfire— or they may not.

*At Boott
Spur, a
heavily-
burdened
hiker admires
Mt. Washing-
ton while the
weather still
permits*

For what is trustworthy, then, we can go back no further than the diaries of European sailors, coasting the New World for fish, treasure, or conquest. Verrazano probably saw Mt. Washington in 1508, when he wrote of "high mountains within the land." Champlain saw it for sure: nearly a century later, he drew a map showing mountains to the west of Casco Bay. The first local color was recorded by an Englishman, Christopher Levett. In 1628 he explored the mouth of the Saco River, on the coast of Maine:

"This river, as I am told by the salvages, commeth from a great mountain called the Christall hill, being as they say 100 miles in the country, yet it is to be seene at the sea-side, and there is no ship arrives in New England, either to the west so farre as Cape Cod, or to the east so farre as Monhiggen [Monhegan Island], but they see this mountaine the first land, if the weather be cleere."

Crystal Hill was not an Indian name, of course, but was devised by English sailors in tribute to its snowy appearance, which they noted even in summer. More often they called it the White Hill. This name was used as early as 1642, when Governor Winthrop of Massachusetts described the first expedition to Mt. Washington:

"One Darby Field, an Irishman living about Pascataquack, being accompanied with two Indians, went to the top of the White hill. He made his journey in 18 days. His relation at his return was that it was about one hundred miles from Saco, that after 40 miles travel he did for the most part ascend, and within 10 miles of the top was neither tree nor grass, but low savins [shrubs] which they went upon the top of sometimes, but a continual ascent upon rocks, on a ridge between two valleys filled with snow, out of which came two branches of Saco River, which met at the foot of the hill where was an Indian town of some 200 people. Some of them accompanied him within 8 miles of the top, but durst go no further, telling him that no Indian ever dared to go higher and that he would die if he went. So they staied there till his return, and his two Indians took courage by his example and went with him. They went divers times through the thick clouds for a good space, and within 4 miles of the top they had no clouds, but very cold. By the way, among the rocks, there were two ponds, one a blackish water, the other reddish [the Lakes of the Clouds]. The top of all was plain about 60 feet square. On the north side there was such a precipice as they could scarce discern to the bottom [the Great Gulf]. They had neither cloud nor wind on the top, and moderate heat. All the country about him seemed a level, excepting here and there a hill rising above the rest, but far beneath them."

Darby Field was an early settler in New Hampshire, a Puritan who went first to Scandinavia and then to the colonies; by 1639 he had settled in Durham. "Pascataquack" was a wide-reaching term in those days, embracing not only the Piscataqua River but also its tributary streams and settlements, including Dover, Durham, and Exeter. I am less able to understand why Governor Winthrop calls Field an Irishman. In fact he appears to have been a native of Boston, England, according to research published in *Appalachia*.

As for his route in June of 1642, that can be deduced from Governor Winthrop's account. Darby Field went along the coast of Maine to the mouth of the Saco, then by canoe to the mountains. Near the present towns of Conway and Fryeburg, the river would have brought him to the Indian territory of Pequawket, with its several villages. One of them could well have been in the vicinity of Glen. Here the Ellis River flows into the Saco, as Governor Winthrop relates. (In twentieth-century terms, this is also where NH 16 flows into US 302.)

From the intervale at Glen, 500 feet above sea level, the easiest and most direct route to the summit would have been along the valley of the Rocky Branch. It climbs steadily from the intervale, rising

3,500 feet in the course of twelve miles. Field would then have bushwhacked for perhaps a mile, gaining another 700 feet in the process. At this point he was standing above treeline on a high, barren ridge, three miles from the summit, with Oakes Gulf on his left and the Gulf of Slides on his right. In the month of June, these might well have been "two valleys filled with snow."*

Walking atop the shrubbery may sound farfetched, but it is one of the details that make this account ring true. Nobody would have invented such a notion. And we have the word of later writers, including Lucy Crawford, that this was a common method of crossing the flanks of Mt. Washington before the trails were cut.

There is one final question: whether Field's was a first ascent. Almost certainly he was the first white man to the summit, but Indians had been living in the neighborhood for time out of mind. Was there not, in all those generations at Pequawket, one red Hillary to make the climb? Believe so if it pleases you. But the Indians were not much given to the conquest of nature. It is a European conceit (and more especially an English one) that God made mountains so that men could climb them.

The trail dipped downward from my breakfast spot, then climbed steadily to treeline, which on the Montalban Ridge is at 4,700 feet. "Treeline" is a relative term. It doesn't mean that you'll find no trees at higher elevations, but that you can no longer trust to them for shelter. The vegetation above this line is dwarfed by wind and snow. At first the trees stand no taller than a man, then they shrink progressively to shoulder height, waist height, knee height; and they grow so intertwined that there is no possibility of forcing a path between them. That is why Darby Field spoke of walking on top of the "savins"—there was no other way he could cross the margin between treeline and bare rock.

Just as a hiker cannot penetrate these thickets, neither can the frost. Snow covers them like an insulating dome, and any branch that sticks through is killed by frost, but enough terminal buds survive that growth will continue next year. Here on the Davis Path, I saw one trunk a foot thick and many that were six inches or more. They must have required a century to reach such a diameter in this climate, yet they were only three feet tall. Nor was it likely that they would grow more than a few inches in the next hundred years.

In many places in the Presidentials, tentsites have been hacked out

---

You may approximate this route by following the Jericho Road out of Glen, then the Rocky Branch Trail, the Isolation Trail to Davis Path, and finally the Davis Path to the summit, a distance of about sixteen miles overall. The North Carolinians had done just that, though they turned back before reaching treeline.

of the scrub. The effect is the same as opening a window to the winter: the canopy is breached, the wind can enter, and the whole thicket is imperiled by frost. To avoid such winter-kill, the Forest Service now forbids camping above timberline anywhere in the White Mountains. The rule is impossible to enforce, however. Hikers do not *plan* to camp above treeline. They are caught there by miscalculation and they pitch their tents regardless, and of course there are no forest rangers at nightfall to tell them otherwise.

I dropped my pack at treeline, to wait for the Nashuan and the Grateful Dead at the customary sign:

STOP
The area ahead has the worst weather in America.
Many have died there from exposure, even in the
summer. Turn back now if the weather is bad.

This warning, posted at every trail leading into the high country, has always given me a delicious shiver of fear.

Here my companions from Isolation Shelter caught up with me. We continued toward Boott Spur together, now clustered and now strung out as the fancy took us. The Grateful Dead was the most independent. The Nashuan was least so, keeping one or the other of us in talking distance all the while.

We were late for the alpine flowers that bloom on Mt. Washington. June is the best month for that. But we saw a few alpine goldenrod, like midget dandelions, and everywhere there were clusters of the five-petaled white flower that is most common above treeline: diapensia. We also saw the grass called Bigelow sedge, which grows by adding cells at the bottom instead of the top, so that it can live through the winter with the barest covering of snow. Diapensia has a different formula for surival. It grows in dense clumps, so low to the ground that it can live even without a protective blanket of snow. This is possible because the chilling effect of the wind is a function of its speed, and because the speed is less at ground level. (Seventy-five miles an hour, six feet above the ground, is reduced to thirty-three miles an hour at the height of six inches.) Thus can the wildflowers thrive in a climate that is the equivalent of northern Labrador, while man can only put on extra garments . . . which we now did. The wind was blowing half a gale when we came up to Boott Spur, and we required jackets even though the temperature was not below sixty degrees.

Boott Spur offers the best possible view of Mt. Washington, the gray cone surmounted by what now resembled cathedral spires— Notre Dame, perhaps, with the Summit House providing the main structure and the television mast its tallest spire of three. We admired them for a time, then pushed along the Davis Path to its junction with the Lawn Cut-off.

Bigelow Lawn was first remarked by John Josselyn, an observant Englishman who came to these shores in 1663. He lived for eight years at Scarboro, Maine, and at some point must have journeyed up the Saco and climbed Mt. Washington. He made this report in *New England's Rarities Discovered*, published in 1672: "Upon the top of the highest of these mountains is a large level or plain of a day's journey over, whereon nothing grows but moss. At the farther end of this plain is another hill, called the Sugar Loaf; to outward appearance a rude heap of massie stones, piled one upon another; and you may, as you ascend, step from one stone to another, as if you were going up a pair of stairs; but winding still around the hill, till you come to the top."

It was a queer approach to mountain climbing, to regard the cone of Mt. Washington as a spiral staircase, but Josselyn was not the only man to think of it. Before World War One there was a grand scheme to build an electric railroad to the summit. The route was actually surveyed in 1911-12, starting at the Cog Railway base station, climbing Mt. Jefferson, then winding two and one-half times around the cone of Mt. Washington. In its twenty-mile journey the train would take in such sights as Tuckerman Headwall, Boott Spur, and the Lakes of the Clouds. Fortunately there was a business recession and the project was abandoned, never to be revived: the hiker on Bigelow Lawn is not required to stop at railroad crossings.

We parted on Bigelow Lawn. The Nashuan and the Grateful Dead turned west for the Crawford Path, where they in turn would separate, one heading south and the other north. I took the direct route to the summit. The Lawn Cut-off wasn't much of a trail. Small cairns marked it at intervals of fifteen feet or so, but otherwise it was just a route across the flinty stones, no more obvious than in John Josselyn's day. I wouldn't have cared to follow it in a cloud-fog such as the one that was now closing upon the summit.

I reached Tuckerman Junction at nine o'clock. A number of trails come together at this place, including Tuckerman Ravine Trail from Pinkham Notch; the junction is marked with a gigantic cairn, much yellow paint, and as many signs as the freeways converging upon Los Angeles. My only view was into Tuckerman Ravine. I saw Hermit Lake a mile away and a thousand feet below, bordered with acres of gravel and scattered buildings, like a shopping center in the early stages of construction. This side of the headwall, five or six hikers were toiling toward me on Tuckerman Ravine Trail. The first to arrive were a young couple and their dog. They continued westward on Tuckerman Crossover, which would take them in time to Lakes of the Clouds Hut, while I stirred myself to climb the last half-mile to the summit.

Almost immediately I was befogged. I was glad of the yellow paint

(highway department yellow, unless I miss my guess) that was splashed on the cairns and even upon the rocks between them. I was also glad to have my walking stick. The wind was thirty miles an hour, enough to throw me off balance while goat-skipping from rock to rock. From Tuckerman Junction to the summit, the trail rises 800 feet in half a mile, which may not sound impressive but nevertheless is very steep indeed. I required an hour to make the grade. Finally I saw a trail-sign through the fog; and then a blue Volvo glided past me, not ten feet away, its engine utterly silenced by the fog. I had come out upon the auto road.

Then I was walking on asphalt. In the parking lot I found half a dozen cars, two motorcycles from Ohio, and a fifty-five-gallon oil drum painted blue and marked with a sign: *water*. (The water is not for hikers but for automobiles, whose radiators often boil en route to the summit.) Dimly I saw a flight of stairs. I mounted them and came to a level space which proved to be the tracks of the Cog Railway. There was no sound or motion anywhere. Crossing the tracks, I found a small gray building and another sign:

THE HIGHEST WIND EVER OBSERVED BY MAN
WAS RECORDED IN THIS BUILDING

The wind was 231 miles per hour; the date was April 12, 1934, and the building was the original Mt. Washington Observatory.

A group of tourists surfaced in the fog. I decided that they must have come from the Summit House, so I walked in that direction. And there it was: Summit House and restaurant, and a railway car with the steam locomotive behind it.

A year or so back, there was a move in the New Hampshire legislature to ban the steam locomotives from Mt. Washington. They burned coal, which was a pollutant, so the Cog Railway should shut down or perhaps convert to diesel fuel. The legislation failed when somebody recalled that 250,000 people visited the summit of Mt. Washington every year: If a normal percentage smoked cigarettes, then the pollution from cigarettes probably exceeded that from the locomotives. So Sylvester Marsh's fantastic contrivance continues to serve the highest peak in New Hampshire, New England, and the entire Northeast. Even North Carolina has nothing like it.

I waited out the fog in the Summit House, where I spent an astonishing $3.10 on a sandwich, a glass of milk, a cup of coffee, and a piece of chocolate cake. I had plenty of company in the restaurant. At least half were hikers, counting both backpackers and goofers, and there were very few happy faces among them. I don't know whether the gloom was the result of the fog, or whether everyone had simply put on his or her city face before entering the Summit House.

There was a souvenir counter in the next room, and an information desk that was doing a brisk business issuing wilderness

A small boy skips along the ties of the Cog Railway, where Tuckerman Ravine Trail comes up from the south

145

permits to hikers. There was a U.S. Postal Service window, also doing a brisk business. ("We don't sell stamps," the girl at the souvenir counter kept telling her customers. "The *post office* sells stamps.") There was a pay phone which advertised itself as the highest this side of the Mississippi, and which was connected to the Gorham switchboard by a radio link. And there were more displays and statistics than a visitor could absorb in an hour. I know: I spent an hour doing just that. Of the information thrown at me in this fashion, I was most taken by the fact that 550,000 gallons of water must be pumped to the summit every summer. The pipeline follows the Cog Railway tracks, a vertical lift of 3,788 feet, and the head of pressure at Marshfield is more than *two thousand pounds* per square inch. . . . I flushed the toilet with something approaching reverence.

Toward noon the fog lifted and I went out to explore. I have been on the summit of Mt. Washington five times altogether, climbing it from the south, west, north, and east. Today's view was as good as any. On a clear day—once a month?—once a year?—they say you can see seventy-five miles from here. I have no reason to doubt the accuracy of this statement, but personally I have never seen farther than Mt. Madison to the north and the Wildcat Ridge to the east. That is enough, believe me. The enchantment of Mt. Washington comes not from the view (the best views in the White Mountains are those that include their tallest summit) but from the presence of an alpine slum so awful as to be beautiful. It resembles a prairie town where two railroads intersect, and where nobody in his right mind would choose to live, except that *somebody* must live there, to serve the railroad. The buildings are graceless and shabby. The railroad tracks are rusting. Antennas sprout everywhere—trussed spires and parabolic reflectors and a television mast which resembles a missile ready for launch. There are foundation stones for buildings long gone, and the chains that once held those buildings to the ground.

*If you can
find it, this
boulder marks
the true
summit of Mt.
Washington:
6,288' above
the sea*

And among all this, behind the Summit House, there is a heap of rock that is the true summit of Mt. Washington. Most visitors climb upon it to have their picture taken. A U.S. Geological Survey marker certifies the altitude (6,288 feet) but it is so worn as to be illegible. The peak-baggers must stand somewhere, after all, and the peak in the end devolves itself into a single rock about three feet square.

When John Josselyn was here, more than three centuries ago, he found the summit to be "a level of about an acre of ground, with a pond of clear water in the midst of it." The pond has since disappeared, or it never was—Josselyn may have misremembered the Lakes of the Clouds. He went on to describe the view: "From this rocky hill you may see the whole country round about; it is far above the clouds, and from hence we beheld a vapour (like a great pillar)

drawn up by the sun beams out of a great lake or pond into the air,
where it was formed into a cloud." Lake Winnipesaukee, perhaps, or
more likely just another cloudbank in a valley. Josselyn closed with a
description of the Northern Presidentials: "The country beyond
these hills northward is daunting terrible, being full of rocky hills, as
thick as mole-hills in a meadow, and cloathed with infinite thick
woods." The wilderness has never been described more powerfully,
though many have tried. Starr King alone devoted sixteen pages to
the attempt.

The weather observatory on Mt. Washington used to have a
"goofer room," which kept the tourists at bay in the high season and
provided shelter for hikers in the winter. (A goofer, in the summit
vocabulary, is anybody who doesn't actually work here. The word
applies equally to the casual tourist and to the veteran alpinist.) But
the visitors became too many, summer and winter alike, and the
goofer room is now closed. Anyone who climbs Mt. Washington in a
blizzard these days will have to make his own way down again, which
in my opinion is how it should be. The winter population on the
summit is four, two men in the observatory and two more at the television transmitter; their work is difficult enough without solacing
winter climbers. It's not as if the climbers weren't warned. In addition
to those infamous Forest Service signs and the cautions in the AMC
Guide, there was this notice in the Summit House: *Hikers, if you
reach the summit and the weather is good, consider yourself lucky; if
the weather is bad or getting worse, that is normal—don't complain
to us. You should have taken time to learn something about where
you were going.*

The other function of the goofer room was to educate the public.
That function is now served more elaborately by the Summit
Museum, next door to the observatory. Apart from the restrooms
(which are free) the museum represents the summit's best value for
the money. Here, for a donation of fifty cents, I learned all that I have
told you about the survival techniques of dwarf fir, diapensia, and
Bigelow sedge. I also learned something about the geology of the
White Mountains, including the fact that a drop of ten degrees in
average temperature would bring the glaciers back to New Hampshire.

The museum also contains a mannikin dressed for winter on Mt.
Washington, a valve from the original Cog Railway locomotive, the
telegraph key used by the first winter inhabitants . . . and a slideboard. The slideboard fascinated me more than anything else. It was,
I judged, about five feet long and one foot wide, with a hand lever on
each side. The levers were brakes. In the nineteenth century, before
the accident rate caused slideboards to be prohibited, workers on Mt.
Washington used these contraptions to descend to Marshfield, three

miles away, straddling the center track of the Cog Railway. The
record time for such a descent was two minutes and forty-five seconds,
or a bit better than sixty-five miles per hour overall. Since the slide-
boarder began at standstill and presumably finished the same way, he
must have been hitting 100 mph by the time he passed over the trestle
known as Jacob's Ladder.

There was also a time when workers would descend on their
shovels, braking with their heels, which resulted in less-spectacular
speeds but even more frequent upsets.

Hypothermia and other hazards

xvi

The Crawford Path takes off between the observatory and the Summit Museum. Indeed, the sign for it is fastened to the north corner of the observatory building. The Crawford Path is the busiest route to the summit; for tourists it offers an excursion to Lakes of the Clouds Hut, 1.4 miles away and 1,238 feet below. The rocks are worn smooth as flagstones.

There were a couple dozen hikers on the trail this afternoon, including two packers bound for the hostel. Lakes is the only AMC hut where all the packing is done downhill. The supplies come up the auto road to the summit, then are carried down the Crawford Path by the hutboys (or hutgirls, as the case may be, but this afternoon both packers were male). I followed them for a time, curious to know what packers talked about while laden with cardboard cartons of flour, vegetables, eggs, and other perishables. They talked about girls. What else? One of them also complained about a stone in his boot, and he sat down to remedy the situation—not as easy as it sounds, since afterward he had to rise again.

Not far below the summit on the Crawford Path, there is a wooden cross beside the trail. It marks the occasion (though not the exact location) of a double tragedy that happened toward the end of July, 1958. As I remember the story, a young couple lost their way in a squall. They were dressed for summer; they had no raingear; they were chilled once by the rain and a second time by its evaporation on the wind. Their blood cooled off like the fluid in a desert water bag, and they died. This process used to be called "suffering from exposure." Now it is called hypothermia, but the symptoms have not changed. First you shiver, then your muscles become stiff, and finally your mind becomes confused, so that any decision you make is probably the wrong one—to sit down and wait out the storm, for example. Hypothermia leads to death soon after the body temperature has dropped to seventy-eight degrees.

Forty-six people have died on Mt. Washington in the little more than a century since it became a major tourist attraction. This is not a large number by European standards: Mount Blanc alone has claimed that many in a single year, and the *annual* death toll in the Alps is something like four hundred. But most Alpine deaths are the result of climbing and skiing accidents. Rock-climbers and ski-mountaineers know the risks, and they incur those risks willingly; but the victims of Mt. Washington were strolling for pleasure. They died not by mischance in a hazardous sport, but because they were unprepared for the weather.

I saw plenty of potential victims that Thursday afternoon in July, hiking the Crawford Path in shorts and polo shirts. The temperature at the summit was sixty degrees and the wind was thirty miles an hour, a combination yielding a chill factor *below freezing.* We weren't aware of the cold. Hiking is fine exercise, and anyhow the sun was shining—for the moment. But a Mt. Washington squall is a sudden beast. If the weather broke we would soon feel the chill, unless we had warm clothing and raingear in our packs.

The first hiker to die in the Presidentials was an Englishman named Frederick Strickland. He left Thomas Crawford's tavern in October 1851, with a companion and a guide. The other two men turned back when they encountered wind and snow on Mt. Clinton, but Strickland pushed on to the summit and attempted to descend by way of the Ammonoosuc Ravine, where his body was found next day in the river. Thus did the Crawfords lose their first guest, although they'd had some arduous moments since Ethan and Abel blazed the Crawford Path in 1819. One of these was the expedition that named Mts. Madison, Adams, Jefferson, and Monroe.

Lucy Crawford told the story in her *History of the White Mountains*, which is not a history at all but a memoir of her remarkable family. It is told in Ethan's words. This technique led nineteenth-century critics to conclude that Ethan "apparently dictated the greater part of the narrative to his wife." More likely, Ethan told the stories so many times that when Lucy decided to write them down, she naturally assumed his voice.

To Ethan's tavern, then, a party came in 1820. The group included Philip Carrigain, who had drawn the first map of the White Mountains; John Weeks of Lancaster, whose descendant would give the family name to the legislation that created the White Mountain National Forest; and five other gentlemen from Lancaster. They loaded Ethan with clothing and provisions for two days. The supplies included "a plenty of what some call 'Black Betts,' or 'O-be-joyful,' as it was the fashion in those days to make use of this kind of stuff, and especially on such occasions." They reached the summit of Mt. Washington on the second day, July 31, 1820. "There they gave names to several peaks," as Lucy wrote in Ethan's voice, "and then drank healths to them in honor to the great men whose names they bore, and gave toasts to them; and after they had all got through, they put it upon me to do the same. . . . The day was fine, and our feelings seemed to correspond with the beauties of the day, and after some hours had swiftly passed away in this manner, we concluded to leave this grand and magnificent place and return to a lower situation on earth."

Drunk as lords, as we must assume, they went down to the Lakes of the Clouds. Having developed a great thirst, they stopped at one of the ponds, "partaking of its waters, until some of us became quite blue, and from this circumstance we agreed to give it the name of Blue Pond. . . . This water so much troubled one of our party, or the elevated situation on which we traveled, fatigue, *or some other cause* [my italics], had such an effect upon him that he could not get along without my assistance; and he being a man of two hundred weight, caused me to make use of all my strength, at times."

Ethan carried other men (and at least one woman) down from the summit. It was to simplify this duty that he built three stone huts above treeline in 1823, providing them with beds of dry moss. He was a sort of one-man Appalachian Mountain Club: trail-blazer, organizer of search-and-rescue misisons, and builder of places of refuge.

153

Lakes of the Clouds Hut is the largest of the AMC's high-country hostels. Its official capacity is ninety, but the capacity has often been exceeded. One night in 1973, two hundred people slept there, with the excess accommodated on and under the tables. There is not much the AMC can do about this situation. Unlike the Mt. Washington Observatory, the AMC is in the hospitality business, and also in the life-saving business. A hiker in trouble can't be turned away, even if his troubles are the result of his own stupidity.

Tonight there would be a full house plus five. I knew Lakes was full because my reservation entitled me only to a backpacker space. (As a service to hikers who couldn't or wouldn't pay for their meals, the AMC kept ten bunks for them at Lakes and gave them a room in which to cook. This option cost $6.50, as against $13.25 for a bed and two meals. But there was no other place to stay in the twelve miles between Mizpah Spring Hut and the Randolph Mountain Club cabins on Mt. Adams, a very long jump even for the likes of Thom Connelly.) I claimed my backpacker space with some difficulty. Lakes had a resident crew of seven, plus drop-in workers from Pinkham Notch Camp and the other hostels. I had to petition three youngsters before finding one who actually worked there. He assigned me to room three. I asked about my chances for dinner, and he told me to ask again at six o'clock. "Let's see how the situation develops," he said. I didn't understand his meaning then, but it soon became clear.

I found room three and made my bed, spreading one blanket for a bottom sheet and two more to cover me. (There is a state law prohibiting guests from sleeping on blankets, and the AMC provides paper sheets—fifty cents—for those who wish to abide by the law. Not many people do. A few days in the mountains makes you very tolerant of such things. Anyhow, the blankets are cleaned on an annual basis, and the season was scarcely a month old.) I bumped my head several times. I had picked the bottom bunk in a tier of three, and there were two such tiers in a room that measured eight feet square.

Then I washed my face for the first time since leaving the Inn Unique—I *saw* my face for the first time since shaving it on Tuesday morning. Hallo there! I washed my socks and smiley-shirt too, and spread them on the rocks to dry. Toward three o'clock the sky turned ugly, so I took the laundry inside. The storm was brief and violent, lashing the hut with such intensity that the windows and roof began to leak. I wondered how many hikers were caught above treeline, on seven square miles of bare rock, without any shelter except the lee of a cairn.

After the squall came the fog, and the hikers began to straggle in. Most of them were wearing ponchos or rain jackets, and some even had rain pants. Others were wet but had planned to spend the night anyhow, and therefore had dry clothing in their packs. But there was a middle-aged couple who had been strolling down the Crawford Path, meaning to have a look at the Lakes of the Clouds, and who had been closer to the hostel than to the summit when the storm overtook them. The woman was wearing open-toed sandals, shorts, a light jersey, and a decorative sweater which she wore across her shoulders, and which she kept tugging together as if to gain some warmth from it. Her husband was wearing street shoes, shorts, and a summer shirt. It was impossible that they could walk back to the summit, dressed as they were and soaked as they were, with a cold cloud-fog streaming on the wind. They would have to spend the night. And they would have to be fed, which among other things meant that I would dine on pemmican.

So I took my dinner out into the fog and ate it in the company of two other backpackers. They too were dining on dry food. They had two police dogs with them, each animal with its own saddlebags, which contained kibble as well as other supplies. Many hikers travel with dogs. Generally they are a nuisance, but I took to these German shepherds because they were carrying their own weight and more. Dogs are objectionable only when they are ornamental. (There was also a poodle at Lakes that evening. He had a cut which I assumed was French, but it was hard to tell because he was so bedraggled from the rain.)

While we backpackers were talking, we heard voices through the fog:

"There's the hut!"

"Where?"

"Right in front of you. Can't you see it?"

A lad with a day pack came out of the mist, closely followed by two packless girls. The girls were so happy to see the bulding that they ran up and touched its shingles, as if to prove it wasn't a mirage. The squall had caught this trio on Bigelow Lawn. They'd come up the Glen Boulder Path to Boott Spur, taking the scenic route to the summit, wearing jeans and cotton jerseys, and only the one day pack among them. Somehow they'd managed to keep their cigarettes dry— smokers always manage to do that—but they had nothing else that was not soaked, and no change of clothes in any event. The girls were in good shape, considering the cold and the fright that had been their companions for the last mile or so. But the boy was stiff. He held his arms away from his body and absolutely straight, as if he had no elbows. Nor did he seem inclined to do anything about it—wrap up in a blanket, for example. He wasn't even happy about paying for dinner.

"You'd better come inside if you want anything to eat," one of the girls told him.

"How much is it?"

"Four-fifty for dinner."

"Two-fifty?"

"No, four-fifty."

"Four-fifty for *each person?* . . . I'll pass."

"You can't. We've signed up for it already."

"Well then, I'll pass breakfast."

As it turned out, there was no room at the dinner tables for these three waifs. They would have to eat later with the crew. Meanwhile I sat down with them, while the guests rattled their cutlery and sang campfire songs and stored away great portions of soup, salad, meat, and vegetables. The atmosphere reminded me of a high-school reunion, loud and cheery and just a little bit desperate, but perhaps that was only because I was on the outside looking in.

The waifs were from Virginia. "We don't have anything like *this,* down there," one of the girls told me. "We started up the Glen Something Trail, you know? And somehow we took a wrong turn and wound up back at the lodge, and then we started up again. Then it started to rain when we were on top, so we decided to head for the hut. We didn't know it was so far. We tried to rest a little bit, but we got so *cold,* so we had to keep moving along. We kept seeing that hut but it always turned out to be a boulder or something."

Between dinner and dessert, the crew put on a little entertainment, and appropriately enough it was a skit about hypothermia. Three of the kitchen crew staggered into the dining room, mocking symptoms from mild to severe, and each received treatment; a hot cup of coffee for the lad who was shivering, a blanket and a girl for the one who was mumbling incoherently, and a jolt of brandy for the third, who promptly keeled over and rolled up his eyes in mock expiration. Then came the serious lecture. Warm drinks for the chilly, with coffee being the best choice because the caffeine acts as a stimulant. For the hiker in an advanced stage of hypothermia, the only remedy is warmth externally applied, and the most available source of heat is another human body. And never, never give coffee or alcohol to anyone who is deep in hypothermia, because the shock will probably kill him.

The three Virginians watched this skit with utter absorption.

The hut was packed this Thursday evening because it was hosting the Annual Range Hike, thirty-six people of all ages and from many states, though mostly from Massachusetts. Why thirty-six? "Because that's the capacity of the smaller huts," one of the leaders told me. He was a man in his fifties with what must have been one of the last Marine Corps crewcuts in North America, no hair longer than a quarter of an inch. He also had a green T-shirt with the legend: *Alpine Guides Club of New England.* And a Swiss Army knife—the outdoorsman's tool chest—clipped to his belt. "Some years," he said, "we have more people, and then we send them out in sections. One year we had a hundred and ten, but this year we got only thirty-six, which is the maximum."

"So when you go to a hut," I said, "any other hiker who wants to spend the night there is out of luck."

"At Zealand and Galehead he is."

"You'd think the AMC would limit the size of a group like that."

"The only reason to limit the size of a group," he told me, "is the competence of its leaders."

"Oh, is that how it's done?"

"Certainly," he said. "Why else would they limit the size of a group?"

So someone else could enjoy the huts. So a lone hiker on the Garfield Ridge wouldn't keep meeting the Range Hikers strung along the trail, thirty-six promenaders on the cruise deck of the Appalachian Trail. *So you won't spoil my view*, for crying out loud.

I talked more with this gentleman, and also with the group's other leader, and in the end I became rather fond of them. Their only sin was their devotion to the hostels, which, as AMC members in good standing, they regarded as group property. They walked the White Mountains as they had walked them ten years ago. They had learned nothing in the interim, except to notice that there were more backpackers on the trail than formerly; since they never stayed at the shelters or campsites, they'd never *met* those backpackers, but only jostled elbows with them in passing. It was as if there were two parallel trails across the backbone of the White Mountains, the one traveled by Thom Connelly and Bobby Ramsey, and the one traveled by the Annual Range Hikers. What could they say to one another, if they did sit down to talk?

The Range Hikers didn't even believe that the backpackers were in the White Mountains to stay. "I give it five more years," one of the leaders told me. "It'll be like water skiing; it'll die out before long. Five years ago everybody was tearing about on water skis, but you don't see it any more. It'll be the same with backpacking."

In tuckerman ravine   xvii

I made an early start from Lakes of the Clouds Hut, heading up the Crawford Path for a few hundred yards, then slabbing the mountainside on Tuckerman Crossover. It was a steep climb to begin with, among boulders that might indeed have suggested buildings to three drenched Virginians. The cloud-fog this Friday morning was as thick as it had been last night. There was no yellow paint on the cairns, either, and they were hard to follow at times. I settled on a policy of keeping the cairns on my left, even if that required me to go over rougher ground. That way I would always know where I stood in relation to the nearest pile of rocks, in case the visibility grew worse.

One time on the Great Gulf Trail, I climbed Mt. Washington in fog so thick that I couldn't tell a horizontal line from a vertical one. The Great Gulf is steep ("such a precipice," as Governor Winthrop related of Darby Field's expedition, "as they could scarce discern to the bottom") and in the fog it seemed absolutely sheer. I clung to the mountain with my hands, fearing that otherwise I would tumble all the way to the bottom. Later, on the cone of Mt. Washington, I spent more than an hour in picking my way from cairn to cairn. I would wait for a rift, dash forward, and as often as not would be obliged to stop halfway because the fog had closed in again.

Today, however, the sky brightened as I walked downhill to Tuckerman Junction. By the time I reached that great, yellow-daubed cairn, Tuckerman Ravine was breaking into view beneath me. It was nine o'clock, and I settled down for breakfast—my second, since I'd already eaten sparsely at the hostel, while waiting to pay my bill. The trouble with pemmican (or its great virtue, depending on whether your goal is to thrive or to survive) is that you can't eat very much at a sitting. Over the past ten days I had developed the habit of snacking every two hours. Even so, I wasn't eating more than eight ounces a day, not counting the meals that had been served up at Lonesome, Greenleaf, and the Inn Unique. In the first week I had exhausted all the notches in my belt; now I was working on the decorative cutouts.

Before finishing this last mouthful of pemmican, I found myself in sunshine. The lip of Tuckerman Headwall was a sharp edge beneath me, and beneath that was the trail leading down into the bowl of Tuckerman Ravine; then the Little Headwall, as it it known to skiers, and finally the raw gravel and the clutter of buildings around Hermit Lake. Blue in the east rolled the summits of the Wildcat Range, with clouds breaking up above them. I wished that the month was April instead of July, and that instead of a walking stick I was equipped with a pair of skis.

Hikers on Mt. Washington can encounter a snowstorm in any month of the year; from October through April they can bet on it. All winter long, snow drifts eastward along the cone of Mt. Washington and is pocketed in Tuckerman Ravine. By April the snow is more than fifty feet deep in the upper bowl. Tuckerman then becomes the ultimate rite of spring for thousands of eastern skiers—the last, best, and most famous wilderness resort this side of the Rockies.

The high season begins in the first or second week of April, just when the lift-served areas close down for lack of snow, and it comes to a climax on Memorial Day. Upwards of three thousand people come to savor that long weekend in Tuckerman Ravine, to ski the fabled headwall or to romp the lower slopes of the bowl, which on a sunny day is the world's largest solar oven, and likewise the world's largest megaphone. You can see the dazzle and hear the chatter while you're still half a mile away.

On one never-to-be-forgotten day in 1969, six thousand skiers and spectators jammed into the bowl of Tuckerman Ravine . . . which has no toilets. (The nearest outhouses are down by Hermit Lake.) Such a crowd will never assemble again, because the custodians of Tuckerman Ravine have decided that their duty is to protect the place, rather than to use it as a coliseum for mountain spectaculars. Since 1969, the AMC and the Forest Service have taken a hard-nosed attitude about who does what in the ravine.

The occasion for that particular crowd was the staging of a race called the American Inferno—a revival, to be more exact. The Inferno was a 1930s classic which involved hiking from Pinkham Notch Camp to the summit of Mt. Washington, then racing back to the highway on skis. The course was just over four miles, the vertical drop was 4,200 feet, and the highlight of course was the headwall of Tuckerman Ravine. The headwall accounted for less than an eighth of the overall descent, but (so to speak) it happened all at once. Most skiers on the headwall come to a full stop after every turn, to gather courage for the next. Such respites are not available to the skier in the middle of a race.

The Inferno was first staged in 1933, with a winning time of about fifteen minutes. A year later, Dick Durrance ran the course in 12 minutes, 35 seconds. Durrance was a notable New Hampshire skier, which in those years meant that he was a notable *American* skier, the laurels not yet having passed to the West. Skiing in 1934 was a New England phenomenon, and more particularly a New Hampshire one.

The Inferno was not run again until 1939, and then only after two postponements. Finally the weather cleared, the snow settled, and forty-four skiers made the long trek to the summit, where they found that the thermometer stood at zero and the wind at sixty miles an hour, for an effective temperature of minus fifty-four. Dick Durrance was among them, of course. So was a certain Toni Matt, who like so many Germans, Swiss, and Austrians had come to teach America how to ski. For a race that included Tuckerman Ravine, Toni Matt had a certain handicap: he had never seen the headwall before he signed up for the Inferno. Or perhaps that ignorance was a virtue, on the theory that foreigners rush in where natives fear to tread. Anyhow, Toni Matt was the man to watch that day.

The racers left the summit at regular intervals, their starting times flashed to Pinkham Notch Camp by radio. Among the early starters was Oscar Cyr, who later wrote an account of the race for *Appalachia*. This is how he described his run down the cone of Mt. Washington, which is a steep slope in its own right: "My course was a series of sweeping snake-like christies, uneventful except for the presence, right through the heart of my every turn, of two straight parallel tracks." The tracks were those of Dick Durrance and Toni Matt. They'd pointed their skis down the cone and run it straight—they'd *schussed* it, as Toni Matt would have said, and as Americans were learning to say—all the way to the lip of Tuckerman Headwall. Here Dick Durrance made the "check" that would slow him down, before he made those precipitous turns on the headwall.

Turns were not Toni Matt's style. "He was seen to come tearing down the cone in one long arc," reported one of the spectators, "and with one swoop that was hardly a check he dropped over the lip of the ravine, *came straight down the headwall,* across the floor, and on down the brookbed to the Sherburne Trail." (Italics added.) The Sherburne Trail was newly cut, a skier's route from Hermit Lake to Pinkham Notch Camp, and it helped the racers to achieve the fabulous speeds that were recorded that day. So did the perfect snow conditions. Toni Matt finished the course in 6 minutes, 29.2 seconds, having averaged thirty-eight miles per hour overall and having cut the previous record almost in half. Dick Durrance finished one minute behind him, and thirty-five other skiers also managed to beat the winning time of 1934.

Speed was one thing. That plunge down the headwall was something else entirely, and it gave Toni Matt an instant place in the pantheon of White Mountains heroes.

Each spring there is an incipient glacier in the upper bowl of the ravine. Snow is heavy, and fifty feet of the stuff weighs so much that the bottom layer fuses into a solid mass of ice. When the snow reaches this depth (as it usually does by the middle of March) the Tuckerman icecap begins to travel. You can't feel the motion, of course, but you can prove it if you like by forming a contour line of stones around the inside of the bowl: the line will droop from day to day, as the icecap slides down to the floor of the bowl.

A week earlier, on the Garfield Ridge, I had been told that Tuckerman Ravine Trail was closed because of ice. I was skeptical, since I was then sweltering in the heat of July, but now I believed it. The trail down into the bowl was dry and firm, but at the bottom there were three great slabs of rotten ice, each the size of a small automobile. These were the remnants of the Snow Arch that forms here every June. Sometimes the arch survives into August, and once it was a popular place for ladies and gentlemen to take their picnic lunches. The man who set the fashion was the indefatigible Starr King. He calculated that the arch was 294 feet long and 15 feet tall, and that the cave it formed was 66 feet deep. At first the picnickers were afraid to enter, but they tested the ice with a hatchet and decided it was "very solid." So they took their baskets inside. Starr King asked: "How can I hope to describe to you the rich surprise of entering this cold, crystal cabin, fashioned by a mountain stream out of the huge, shapeless quarry that is deposited and hardened there by the winter storms?" After that question—and a three-page answer—the picnic itself comes as something of an anti-climax. We know only that it included both pie and cheese, and that the toasts weredrunk in "pure ice-water fresh from February."

That was in the 1850s. In 1886 a lad from Boston was killed when the Snow Arch collapsed on him; eight years later, fifty hikers went through the arch just before a hundred-foot section fell on the trail. These developments put an end to the custom of picnics at this spot. The Forest Service now posts a warning sign beside the trail and the AMC Guide declares: "Persons are cautioned not to approach too near the arch, and *under no consideration* to cross or venture beneath it, as one death and several narrow escapes have already resulted."

The arch forms at the tightest curve of the bowl, where the head-wall completes its drop and sweeps out in more gentle fashion. It is here that the snow accumulates to its greatest depth.* The headwall thaws first because it is exposed to the sun, and by the middle of June it is running with water, inspiring nineteenth-century admirers to name it "The Fall of a Thousand Streams." These streams, uniting lower down, undermine the icecap and create the arch.

I hiked down to the settlement at Hermit Lake. The first building along the trail was the Forest Service headquarters, a creosote-brown cabin with green shutters; beyond it were the latrines. They were being renovated this morning by two boys and three girls in red hard-hats. I especially admired a small blonde who wielded her hammer with contemptuous skill, like a carpenter to the blue collar born. I wanted to ask where she'd learned to swing a hammer like that. But she was busy—the busiest of the crew, in fact—and Mt. Washington seemed to have taken away my appetite for talking to strangers. To this young woman, I was just another pedestrian on a trail that was already too crowded.

Across the trail was the construction site which, from Tuckerman Junction, had suggested a gravel parking lot. A warming hut for skiers would be erected here, though nobody was working on it this

---

I can't find a trustworthy figure. The depression-era New Hampshire: A Guide to the Granite State *suggested that it could reach "200 or 300 feet" and added that "in many summers the sun is unable to melt the snow down to this underlying part." If so, our winters are indeed not what they used to be. The Forest Service rangers in Tuckerman Ravine say that eighty-five feet has been the maximum in recent years.*

Friday morning. The AMC has not been lucky with its buildings in Tuckerman Ravine. (Actually they are owned by the Forest Service and leased to the AMC.) They keep burning to the ground, the most recent one because of a leak in the propane gas line. The replacement will not provide the hot coffee and fat cheeseburgers which once were part of the spring-skiing ritual, and which earned for the old warming hut its nickname of "Howard Johnson's." Food service was discontinued in the spring of 1971, as yet another turn of the screw in Tuckerman Ravine. The new building will have a sheltered sundeck for the skiers, but the interior will be given over to sleeping quarters and a kitchen for the crew that manages the Hermit Lake complex. Meanwhile the crew (manager, assistant, and cook) was living in a brown wall tent nearby.

Camping is strictly regulated at Hermit Lake, and has been since the busy days of the late 1960s, when upwards of five hundred people slept overnight in the ravine. The sanitary facilities couldn't handle them. Neither could the vegetation, which even at this altitude (about 4,000 feet) is the equivalent of Arctic tundra. Tenting was banned, and campfires too, and the shelter spaces were sold at Pinkham Notch Camp on a first-come basis. More recently this policy has been eased a bit, and a few tenters are tolerated while snow is on the ground.

For a time there were nine lean-tos at Hermit Lake, but fire destroyed one of these as well, and now the overnight capacity is eighty-six. Skiers compete fiercely for these spaces. On a Saturday in April or May, if you are not in line before seven o'clock in the morning, your chances of obtaining an overnight permit are very slim. But things are more relaxed in the summer, at least in July. The shelters had been only half full the night before.

All told, from Tuckerman Junction to Pinkham Notch Camp, I met thirty-eight people upward bound: an average of one hiker for every three minutes I spent on the trail. What surprised me was not their number but how fastidious they were. I spotted the odd orange peel or cigarette butt, but nothing comparable to the trash I've seen in the mountains of Europe. Americans have a fondness for exaggeration. We accuse ourselves of polluting like no other people on the face of the earth, yet Tuckerman Ravine—one of the most popular routes to our most popular summit—is tidy enough to put a Swiss to shame.

Wilderness incorporated

Pinkham is the broadest of the White Mountain notches, and it was a long while before anyone paid much attention to it. Starr King, who had so much to say about everything else, and who circled Mt. Washington restlessly for several hundred pages before taking us to the summit, doesn't mention it at all. (He does refer to "a clearing in the Pinkham woods," but that is in connection with a legend about the origin of the Peabody River. "The inmates of an Indian cabin . . . were roused in the night by a singular and dreadful noise," which proved to be a river bursting from the hillside, sweeping the cabin away.) Neither does Frederick Kilbourne's history of the White Mountains, published in 1916, contain more than a single reference to Pinkham Notch—and that one set in parentheses. The notch, until very recently, was merely a high spot in the road.

The road was begun in 1774. It was still under construction when Jeremy Belknap made his expedition to Mt. Washington ten years later, and apparently it wasn't completed for another ten years at least, for the sons of Joseph Pinkham are said to have worked on it. The Pinkhams didn't reach the North Country until 1790. They came up from the seacoast in the dead of winter, with all their worldly goods in a sled. The sled was drawn by a pig in harness. It is astonishing how many pioneers made their moves in the wintertime. They weren't being perverse: as farmers, they were obliged to stay in one place between the sowing and the harvest, else they would have nothing to eat for the year.

Here, in the region where Joseph Pinkham struggled through the drifts with his family, his sled, and his able-bodied pig, the AMC now operates Pinkham Notch Camp. The name is a classic of understatement. I checked in at the main lodge, for all the world like Mr. Tourist at the Holiday Inn, and the receptionist gave me a towel and a key. A key! "I think your bed will be made up by now," she told me.

And so it proved to be. I walked along a crushed-stone path to the Joe Dodge Center, which was not nearly so awful as Florence Morey had led me to expect. It was rather nice, in fact, a two-story building in board-and-batten style. The boards were stained the inevitable creosote brown, but the architect—and perhaps this was what had troubled Mrs. Morey—had dared to include vertical bands of white plywood where the windows were set in. The locals seemed to have accepted the building with no great fuss. They had even given it a nickname, as all things are nicknamed by the youngsters of the AMC: Dodge Lodge. I found a tiled entryway, a hall carpeted wall to wall in russet, and room 102 with four bunks neatly made up with blankets and sheets. There was a thermostat, too, and an Anderson Thermopane window whose lock required all my ingenuity to open. And a little orange bureau and pegs for hanging up my clothes. And—nicest touch of all—each bunk had a light switch whose location was marked by a glowing neon dot, and which controlled a fluorescent lamp above the pillow.

There was a shower down the hall. It was tiled like the entryway, with a temperature-control valve even more complex than the window lock. I was in there ten minutes before I got the hang of it. No matter. Frigid or scalding, it was all refreshing, the first shower I'd had in almost two weeks, and only the second time I had bathed in hot water.

Then I set out to explore Dodge Lodge. At the southern end I found a two-story library, a hushed place which rather pointedly had no ashtrays. The reading matter was richer than that of the huts, whose collections are generally limited to old guestbooks, back copies of *Appalachia*, and religious tracts left by those mysterious people who have put bibles in every motel room in the nation. Here there were files of the *National Geographic* going back to 1918, and bound volumes of the *Alpine Journal* going back to 1863. There were current magazines, too, and a selection of books that for some reason included Allen Drury's *Advise and Consent*. On a balcony overhead, reached by a spiral stairway, there was a table for chess and checkers.

The north end of the building was very different. Here there was a lounge with ancient maroon armchairs and couches, braided oval rugs, a brick fireplace, an old trestle table, and a piano. I had seen those sagging couches before, in the lounge of the former dormitory building—and slowly it dawned on me that this *was* the old dormitory, or part of it, and that the architect had worked it in so neatly that I hadn't noticed the trick from the outside.

Downstairs I found another clubroom, called the Rathskeller, though I had no way of knowing if rathskeller-like activities were allowed to happen there. (AMC Old Boys lifting steins of beer in the cellar of the Dodge Lodge?) I also found a portrait of an outdoorsman with a golfing cap, a ruddy complexion, and a cigarette clipped between his teeth: Joe Dodge himself.

This tribute was published in *Appalachia:* "Joe Dodge was a builder, skier, hiker, a husband and father, weatherman, fisherman, forecaster. He was a White Mountain Man, and he was a strong man. He pioneered in a 20th Century sort of way, charting his own path, but never straying so far from it that others would not happily (though often cussing and weary) tread after him." He also did some cussing on his own account. Joe Dodge stories are invariably full of dashes to indicate language unfit to print, as when someone suggested adding yet another ell to one of the high-country hostels: "You built a dingle on the ——— shack two years ago," Joe replied; "last year you built a dingle on the dingle, but to build a dingle on the dingle on the dingle is just ——— foolishness!" It is said that people used to go to Pinkham Notch Camp just to hear Joe Dodge swear.

He was twenty-three when he went to work for the AMC, a former radioman for the U.S. Navy and the Boston-to-Portland steamship line. Two log cabins had been built in the notch in the summer of 1920, and Joe was actually the second hutmaster to take up residence there. He was also the cook, the accountant, and the man who tramped to the high-country hostels (Lakes, Madison, and Carter) to ensure that they were not vandalized in the spring and fall. For the first five years, this was a three-season job. Then, in 1926, the AMC hired Joe to manage Pinkham Notch Camp in the winter as well. "By Thanksgiving time," he reported in *Appalachia*, "the camp was pretty well secured for the winter and we stocked supplies from Berlin and Boston. Most of the meats we wrapped in heavy brown paper and froze them hanging in the old barn, and as soon as there was sufficient snow we made a cache in the snow and covered the meats with rocks so the animals could not get to them." The animals were mostly porcupines. There were so many porcupines at Pinkham Notch Camp that Joe christened it "Porky Gulch"—a name still sometimes heard, and one so common in the early years that it appeared on incoming mail. Joe supplemented the camp's income with the twenty-eight-cent bounty for porcupines, which he killed at the rate of a dozen a day.

Even with the bounties, Pinkham Notch Camp lost $119 that first winter. It was a lonely season for Joe, who used his radio skills to court a girl in Brookline, Mass., and to order a ring for her. The radio was his only link with civilization, and remained so for several winters. Anyone who visited Pinkham Notch Camp in those years, after snow was on the ground, had to trek from Jackson on the south or Gorham on the north.

Joe Dodge presided over the creation of the AMC hut system. The three pioneering hostels were already in place when he came to the North Country, but it was Joe who extended the chain south and east to Franconia Notch. This he did in 1929 and 1930, surveying sites at Zealand Falls, Mt. Galehead, and Mt. Lafayette. In 1929, also, the AMC took over the operation of a fishing camp at Lonesome Lake. So when the new hostels were open for business, a strong hiker could cross the White Mountains and sleep every night in an AMC bunk. It was such a good system that it remained unchanged for a generation, until Mizpah Spring Hut was built near Mt. Clinton in 1964. By that time, Joe was five years into retirement.

He pioneered spring skiing in Tuckerman Ravine; he organized the American Inferno and timed the early races; he installed the hydro-electric system which supplied Pinkham Notch Camp with power from 1939 to 1960; he was the driving force behind the Mt. Washington Observatory; and he collected an honorary degree from Dartmouth on the same platform as Robert Frost—not bad for a man who went to sea at the age of fifteen. He died on October 28, 1973. To mourn him, in the words of one of them, Joe Dodge left "about as many friends as there are trees in New Hampshire."

It's a far cry from Porky Gulch to Wilderness Incorporated, which is the dominant impression at Pinkham Notch Camp today. This sign adorns its entrance, between NH 16 and the parking lot:

PINKHAM NOTCH CAMP
of the
APPALACHIAN MOUNTAIN CLUB
Center of Hiking and Skiing in the
WHITE MOUNTAIN
NATIONAL FOREST
Meals & Lodging — Trail Information
Mountain Hospitality for All

Wilderness
Incorporated

The hospitality is provided at Dodge Lodge, of course, and also at the Trading Post next door. The Trading Post is a Topsy-grown building which, depending on your angle of approach, resembles a comfortable old cabin or the base lodge at a ski resort. It contains the public facilities of Pinkham Notch Camp, including a sales desk, a dining room, and coin-operated showers.

Behind the Trading Post (and not quite visible from it) the real work of Wilderness Incorporated is done in what looks like a converted highway-department garage. There are two of these buildings. They have the long and boxy lines of old barracks, with much grass and little gravel, and with trucks continually moving out at the behest of a man with a clipboard. Altogether, the atmosphere evokes an army depot in wartime.

Where Joe Dodge once labored alone, the AMC North Country division now boasts a summer payroll of 135. Six of these are managers. The bed-and-board operation at Pinkham has its own full-time supervisor, though he still bears the homely title of hutmaster. There is another manager for the hut system overall, two for research, two for trails and campsites, and yet another for "operations," whatever that may entail. Finally and inevitably, there is an executive director to manage all the managers.

Then there's a program director, who plans the educational activities at Pinkham Notch Camp: clinics for cross-country skiers; workshops for photographers and for those who want to improve their skills with map and compass; lessons in how to rescue the injured and how to make your own backpacking gear; seminars in natural history, astronomy, geology, and winter ecology; a weekend devoted exclusively to mushrooms, and another devoted to lichens, mosses, and liverworts. (A liverwort is not a sausage but a mosslike plant that grows on tree trunks and in other damp places.) For those of us who resist education, the program director also schedules an occasional film or folk dance.

While I stood on the margin of NH 16, trying to visualize the Porky Gulch of fifty years ago, I was visited by three wonders in a row. The first of these was an antique-car rally. They came up the highway from the south: a Model A Ford, a Rolls Royce with the monogram in

171

red (signifying that Mr. Rolls—or was it Mr. Royce?—was still alive when it left the factory), a Packard touring car, and a number of 1940s models that in my boyhood had been considered first-class transportation for middle-class families. Now they qualified for antique-car plates, and I find it difficult to say how strange that made me feel. I was still pondering the difference a quarter-century can make, in men and machines, when I realized that a young hiker was signaling me from across the road. With lip movements more than with voice, he said: *Look at the moose!*

In seventy-five miles of walking, I'd encountered nothing larger than a spruce grouse and a snowshoe hare. But now, hard by Wilderness Incorporated and a three-lane highway, a cow moose was grazing in a pond across the way. She was gray and ungainly, as out of place as that Packard touring car, and she realized it soon enough. Another hiker came out of the woods on Lost Pond Trail. The moose reared her big head, pulled her hooves from the mud with a great sucking noise, and galloped off into the underbrush. I was so enchanted that I never thought to take the camera out of my shirt pocket.

Then the third marvel. There is a tall pole at the entrance to Pinkham Notch Camp, just in front of the hospitality sign, with an American flag duly snapping in the breeze. While I stood beneath it, I was bothered by a smell familiar to all countrymen: sweet-and-sour marsh gas, the signal that a septic tank has quit working. As it happened, I knew where the Pinkham sewerage system was located. The last time I'd been here, the parking lot had been half torn up for the installation of a new drainage field, yet the smell was noticeable only at the flagpole. I couldn't understand that.

But when I turned back for Dodge Lodge, I noticed a large exhaust fan half-buried in the grass. It was connected by six-inch white pipe to the base of the flagpole—which wasn't exclusively a flagpole, as I now realized. It was also a vent for the sewer system.

I napped before dinner, two and one-half hours by Sally's watch. Then I walked over to the Trading Post and joined the line that had formed in the lobby. There weren't many backpackers in the dinner line: the folks with meal tickets were not very different from those you'd meet at the Eastern Slopes Inn, though more casually dressed and more lined from the sun and the wind. They included children and grandparents, and they even included a black man. I decided to sit with him and to pry a little. Hiking, like skiing, tends to be a lily-white sport in these parts, to such a degree that I am still startled by the sight of a black hiker. Perhaps the self-inflicted punishment of mountaineering has a special attraction for the Anglo-Saxon temperament. (Hillary assaulted Mt. Everest *because it was there;* Muhammad Ali had a more sensible motive for battling Joe Frazier.)

More likely, the mountains are just too expensive for most of the minority. The lad from Scarsdale—he who objected to paying a dollar at a supervised campsite—was decorated with at least $500 worth of clothing and equipment. That's the entrance fee for the wilderness experience, if you follow the blandishments of the mountain specialty catalogs.

I should have known: my dinner companion worked for the AMC in Boston. In this era of "affirmative action," the office on Joy Street could hardly have managed without a black employee. He was Charlie Ruvin, who ran the AMC's Youth Opportunities Program, training group leaders from Roxbury and other poor neighborhoods of Boston. The AMC also lent a hand with equipment. The upshot was that the Roxbury Boys' Club could set off for the mountains and the same kind of wilderness therapy as that offered by Random Backpacking. (At Guyot Shelter, by the way, all four campers had been white.) But while Random Backpacking was intended as a cure for juvenile delinquency, the Youth Opportunities Program served more like preventive medicine.

Whether any of this does any good, I wouldn't hazard a guess. It's possible that backpacking develops leadership, independence, an appreciation of the wide world, and all manner of good things. It's also possible that when the lad from Roxbury meets the lad from Scarsdale, he'll go home angrier than before.

After dinner I joined the scheduled nature walk, led by Lilly and Cindy in green AMC CROO T-shirts. I learned that the broad, soft leaves of hobblebush are the White Mountain substitute for toilet paper; that the leaves of the bluebead lily can be eaten in a salad, tasting for all the world like cucumber; and that mountain shamrock is good for slaking thirst, since it has a tart lemon taste that makes you salivate. I also learned, after a generation in and around the woods of New Hampshire, a foolproof test for distinguishing spruce from fir. Grab a twig; the tree is spruce if the needles are prickly, fir if they are soft. Thank you, Cindy. I've been wondering about that for most of my lifetime.

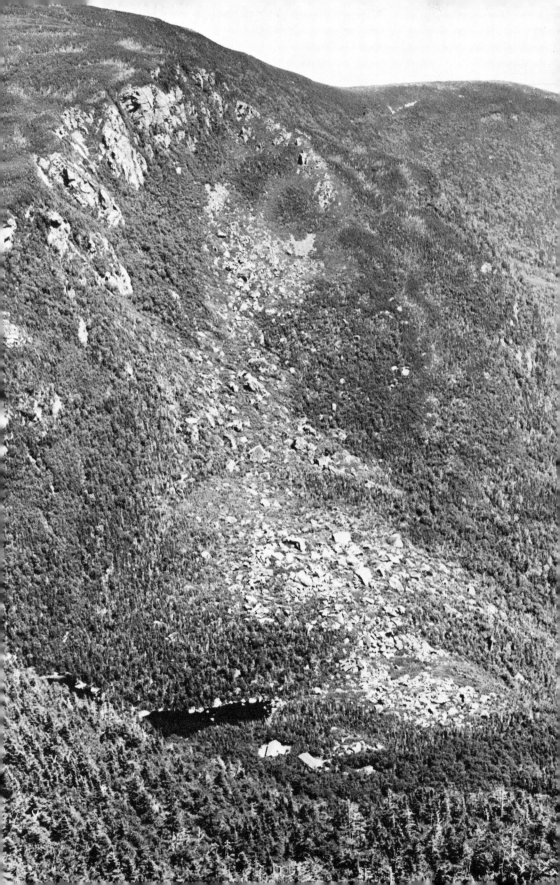

Carolyn did it...   xix

From Pinkham Notch Camp to Carter Notch Hut, the distance is about seven miles over the Wildcat Ridge. I had traveled farther in a day, but Saturday's march would be high ground all the way, over peaks so numerous that they are identified by letters instead of names. So I paid my bill before breakfast and left my pack waiting on the porch, to give myself the earliest possible start. (Seven forty-five, as it happened. The family-style breakfasts of the AMC make no concession to the hiker who likes to rise at dawn.) I crossed NH 16 to the Lost Pond Trail, where I'd seen the cow moose yesterday, then crossed the Ellis River on another fine footbridge. I walked along the east bank of the Ellis for a mile, until the Wildcat Ridge Trail began its climb to Summit E. On the opposite bank a girl was tending a campfire in front of a yellow tent. I said hello. She told me that it had been a cold night. She was breaking at least four rules of the Pinkham Notch Scenic Area—tenting, building a fire, camping beside a river, camping near a highway— but we didn't go into that.

At Pinkham Notch Camp I had learned that the barometer was forecasting "change," that the temperature was sixty degrees, and that the wind was coming out of the northeast at twenty miles an hour. More to the point, I'd seen the Wildcat Range enveloped in clouds. Their bottoms were more yellow than gray, which at home would have meant that a rainstorm was in progress. Here in the mountains it apparently meant nothing at all. I began to climb the ledges of Wildcat E, the wind blowing fiercely at my back, but without a drop of rain to trouble me.

The ledges were fun. From below they seemed a smooth face of rock, but on close inspection they always proved to offer handholds and footholds to make the climbing easy. It was a nice way to go up a mountain, and for the first time I understood the special joys of rock-climbing. I still wouldn't dream of attacking the Cannon Cliffs with rope, carabiners, and pitons, but I can appreciate why others might find it a challenge and a pleasure. The higher I climbed, the better the outlook became, until I topped the final ledge at ten o'clock. There I put on a sweater and admired the view into Pinkham Notch, with the AMC buildings clustered almost directly below me. Through a cleft in the mountains I saw the base of Tuckerman Headwall, black and seemingly vertical, but cut short by a cloud that formed a contour line at perhaps 4,500 feet. Above this cloud there was a ribbon of blue sky. Then began the yellow-bellied clouds that still hovered over the Wildcat Ridge. Pinkham Notch Camp was in sunlight, though, and the shadows of my clouds moved rapidly through the notch.

Since leaving the Inn Unique on Tuesday, I had walked under a cloud (or in one) almost all the way, but every time I reached a summit the sun broke through. The miracle was repeated on Wildcat E. Even better, the sun continued to shine as I marched along the ridge to Wildcat D, where I heard the clanking of machinery and the steady whine of a diesel engine.

The national forest is a "land of many uses," as the signs proclaim. Skiing is one of these uses, along with hiking, snowmobiling, the timber harvest, hunting and fishing, water storage . . . as many uses as there are lobbyists in Washington to exploit the wilderness for pleasure or profit. Among these special and often conflicting interests, the ski industry seems to be losing its former influence, probably because it is so visible. Visibility no longer pays. J.E.

Henry's successors are clearcutting great swaths of the White Mountain National Forest, but not where we can see them. At a ski resort the mess is immediately apparent: parking lots, base lodge, service buildings, uphill lifts, trails and open slopes, and often a summit lodge as well. Anyone with the stamina to drive around the mountains can view the ski resorts, but only a bushwhacker knows what the woodcutters are doing in the back of beyond.

Each year the national forest gives up six million cubic feet of timber. In terms of firewood, that's enough to heat ten thousand drafty farmhouses like mine, yet I crossed the White Mountains without once hearing the sound of a chainsaw. Wildcat D, on the other hand, was the second ski resort along my route.

I left the trail to visit the summit lodge, which I reached at ten-thirty or so. The egg-shaped gondola cars were already coming up the mountain, each with two passengers, and the restaurant was just opening for the day. I went inside for coffee and a jelly doughnut. The restaurant was also a gift shop, stocked with "Indian" trinkets and other souvenirs. A boy wielded a mop, children and parents wandered in, and the counter girl chattered nonstop to all of us. She told me that if I followed the tourist path to the observation tower, I would find myself once again on the Wildcat Ridge Trail. She was correct. The first step to the platform, in fact, was placed athwart the trail, so that every Through Hiker on the Appalachian Trail was obliged to plant his foot upon it. There was a rubbish can as well.

I spent an hour on the platform, waiting for Mt. Washington to emerge from the clouds, which it did at twelve o'clock. Meanwhile I talked to the tourists. One man told me that he had driven up the auto road to Mt. Washington, a few hours earlier, when the temperature was thirty-five degrees and the wind seventy-five miles an hour. "I opened my door to take a picture," he said, "and it was all I could do to get it closed again. So we decided to come up here instead." I played the tour guide for him: Boott Spur on the left, then Tuckerman Ravine, then Lion Head and Huntington Ravine. We could even see the footpaths leading up to Boott Spur and Lion Head.

I was in no hurry, because I had a reservation at Carter Notch Hut, but eventually I ran out of listeners. So I moved along to the next summit eastward. There I began to meet other hikers, all of them bagging the Wildcats on day trips from the highway. (Of the five peaks along the ridge, only the first and last qualify for the Four Thousand Footer Club. Wildcat E is 4,041 feet above sea level; the main summit is 4,397. Summits B through D are tall enough but they don't meet the test of rising 200 feet above an intervening col.) From Wildcat C there is a gorgeous view of the Maine mountains, but so arranged that I couldn't see the valley that I would enter tomorrow, on the last leg of my trip. Neither was it visible from the main summit, where I spent a lazy half-hour on the overlook, with Carter Notch

Hut almost directly beneath my feet. The eastern face of Wildcat is one of the steepest in the mountains. The trail drops one thousand feet in eight-tenths of a mile, and a good part of that distance is taken up in switchbacks. As an avalanche would go, the trip can't be more than half a mile.

Eastward was the boulder-strewn face of Carter Dome, which stood between me and the Wild River valley. Because of that obstruction I would be walking south tomorrow morning. Then I would turn east and climb through Perkins Notch, 2,586 feet, and then it was all downhill to Hastings, Maine, where Sally would meet me in two days' time.

I met more hikers on the downward pitch. First there were two boys, who collapsed by the side of the trail and begged to know how far it was to the top. "Not far," I told them—the obligatory answer to this question, and one that is seldom honest.

Later I met the girls. "Did you see two guys up ahead?" the first one asked.

"Yes," I said, "and they just sat down to rest."

"I'm glad to hear it," she said, then gave me the canteen she was carrying. "Would you mind putting this into my pack?" I did so, sliding the canteen into the back pocket, but there was no way to fasten it in place. It would fall out again the next time she leaned forward. I suspected that she was doing a lot of leaning, to grapple Wildcat with her hands. Her pack was new and grossly overloaded. That's the trouble with a modern packframe. It carries so much weight, and carries it so comfortably, that a novice hiker seldom starts out with less than forty pounds on board. That's too much by half, in my opinion. It seems light when you first put it on, but the weight is the same no matter how cleverly it is distributed, and your legs must carry it to the summit. The old-fashioned rucksack protected its wearer from this kind of folly. Nobody in his right mind would put forty pounds into a rucksack, for his shoulder muscles would be aching by the time he was out of the parking lot.

I reached the hostel at three o'clock. Carter was built in 1914, which makes it the oldest of the standing huts. (There has been a hut on Mt. Madison since 1888, but not the same one.) It is a small stone cabin, which sixty years ago contained all facilities for thirty-six people. They must have slept in tiers and dined in shifts, because now the hut is considered just large enough for the kitchen, the common room, and the crew's quarters. The guests sleep in two detached bunk-houses built in 1963. The new buildings are fashioned from plywood, which makes them very attractive to porcupines: the porkies have gnawed every accessible panel in order to taste the glue.

At the other hostels, I'd felt like an intruder at a private party, standing forlorn at the desk until somebody could spare the time to see what I wanted. At Carter things were managed differently. The

cook wiped his hands upon his apron, came over to me, and said: "I'm Joe Waterman." I shook hands in astonishment. But this was the policy at Carter Notch Hut, apparently, for the same thing happened with the lad who signed me in. "I'm Dave Hazen," he said, pushing a purple-and-red hat to the back of his head. Then it was the hutmaster's turn: "I'm Carolyn McManus." I didn't meet the fourth member of the crew. She'd just hiked down the Nineteen Mile Brook Trail to attend a rock concert in North Conway.

Dave Hazen proved to be the master of ceremonies. After dinner he swept us away on his version of a nature walk, which made up in joviality what it lacked in factual content. Dave was a bit vague when it came to the flora of the notch. "Oh, that's a moss or something," he would say when challenged about the undergrowth. And he referred to the scrub trees as pine, when even I could see that they were fir or spruce. (Both, as I determined by my new-found test.) They were thoroughly dwarfed, even at an altitude of 3,400 feet, because the north wind comes strong and cold through Carter Notch, giving it a climate very like the upper reaches of Mt. Washington. This was another upside-down treeline, such as I had seen from Guyot Shelter and along the Bondcliff Trail.

Somebody wanted to know how the propane gas tanks arrived at the hostel. "Oh those," Dave said, pushing his purple-and-red hat to a new position at the back of his head. "A helicopter brings them in, during the winter, and drops them on the pond."

"And you carry them to the hut?"

"No," Dave said. "Carolyn does it."

"Carolyn?"

"They only weigh two hundred pounds," Dave told him. "Empty, they weigh a hundred pounds, so then she carries them two at a time." He explained that the empty cylinders were muscled over here to the Ramparts, the boulder-strewn area above the hostel. They were lashed together in groups of six, with steel cable, and with a steel ring fastened to the parcel. Then a helicopter came in and grabbed it with a sky hook. "The pilot is *that good,*" Dave told us, holding an imaginary ring over his head while an imaginary helicopter came down and skewered it. "Now!" he said, briskly rubbing his hands, returning to the business that had brought us here to the Ramparts. "Can anybody tell me how these boulders got here?"

"Carolyn did it!" shouted one of the guests.

Dave enjoyed that as much as he enjoyed his own jokes. "Yeah," he said, probably storing it up for future use. "Carolyn did it!" Then he confessed that the boulders had actually been split off from the western face of Carter Dome, by earthquake or frost action, either one. We gazed in awe at the ledges on Carter Dome. There was one boulder especially—a classic hanging rock—that looked as if it might follow the others at any moment. "Pulpit Rock," Dave said.

Somebody wanted to know when it was likely to fall. Dave studied the cliff. "Don't worry about it," he said at last. "Carolyn and I climbed up there last week, and we put a good wedge under it."

Then he took us through the rock caves. As the boulders had tumbled down into Carter Notch, they had formed a honeycomb of holes and passages which twisted and turned beneath the surface. Some of the caves still had ice at the bottom. In June, when the summer crew had arrived, they found that the propane refrigerator was out of order, and for three weeks they'd stored the food in these natural iceboxes.

Not all the guests could squeeze through the passages in the rock— or wanted to, for that matter. The children were the most enthusiastic and I was a close second. As with rock-climbing, so with caving: I'd never understood the attraction until this Saturday. I was terribly disappointed when Dave told me that my longest excursion underground was ten feet in and ten feet out again.

Among its other distinctions, Carter Notch Hut was the only one in which smoking was prohibited. Carolyn may have been responsible for the no-smoking signs, as she seemed to be responsible for everything else in Carter Notch, but I suspect that it was Dave Hazen's idea. He did not approve of cigarettes. We were standing outside the hut when Dave cleared his throat and looked me in the eye. "About your smoking, sir!" he said. I knew what was troubling him. There was a squashed cigarette on the ground nearby. I explained that it wasn't my brand, and that anyhow I kept my butts with me as I traveled. To prove it, I pulled the baggie from my hip pocket and showed him the collection. "Dynamite," he said, satisfied that I was innocent.

Then he and Carolyn went into a little vaudeville act. Earlier in the day, on the Nineteen Mile Brook Trail, they'd come across a pack of cigarettes. It is impossible to lean over while carrying an AMC packboard—eighty pounds balanced above your head—and if you try to reach the ground by hunkering, then you have the very difficult task of standing up again. So Carolyn scooped up the litter with the toe of her boot, like a soccer ball, and Dave Hazen caught it on the fly.

"What did you do with them?" one of the guests asked.

"Burned them in the stove."

"You should have kept them," said the guest, who was smoking like a sailor, the cigarette cupped in his hand. "You could have sold them for a dollar apiece to the guy who lost them."

"No," Dave said. "Anyhow, there are better things to smoke than cigarettes."

While we were clowning in this fashion, three hikers came up the trail from the north. One lad had tent poles sticking from his pack, looking just like a mobile rocket launcher—a score of aluminum projectiles that could only have belonged to a family-sized umbrella tent. Even more strange, one of his companions was carrying two kerosene lanterns. They were the same red lanterns that farmers used to carry, or railway brakemen, with a glass globe to protect the flame from the wind.

They wanted to know where they could pitch their tent. So Dave became the hutman-educator, explaining that this was a Restricted Use Area and that no camping was allowed within a half-mile of the hostel. "If you go about a mile down the Wildcat River Trail," he said, pointing to the south, "you'll find a campsite already cleared. It's not cool—we don't like to see campsites along the trail—but it's legal." The hikers thanked him, waited until he went back to the kitchen, then returned in the direction from which they had come.

After they were gone, the rest of us talked about similar wonders we had seen along the trail. I told about the Hamden Four, who had made it to Eliza Brook Shelter with a road map. Then somebody told about the family that was hiking the White Mountains with "the bare essentials," including, among other things, a gasoline lantern and a two-burner gasoline stove. I topped that with my friend from Nashua, with his canned goods and five-quart water bag and six-shot revolver. The revolver made a great hit, but it paled beside the family that had been seen in Tuckerman Ravine with a pet llama from Peru. The llama was their pack animal.

Next morning early, I walked down to the pond, hoping to surprise a beaver at breakfast. Instead I found the three hikers. They were sleeping beside the trail, not four feet from a sign that said NO CAMPING. Perhaps out of respect for the sign, they hadn't set up their umbrella tent. They stirred in their sleeping bags when I came by, so I asked where they'd come from and whither they were bound. "We're going out to the highway," they said. "Yesterday we went up to the top of Carter Dome and then down to here." Which made a total weekend distance of five miles . . . which was just about right, considering the burden they were carrying.

I walked back to the hut, wondering if any of the three would ever come back to the mountains. Probably not. Nor would the three Virginians who'd been soaked on Mt. Washington, nor the Hamden Four, nor the Girl Scouts from Illinois, nor (though I had some hope for him) the pistol-packing construction worker from Nashua.

I admired their spirit, if not their common sense, for at least they were trying to be independent and to take the wilderness on its own terms. That couldn't be said of the Annual Range Hikers, trooping from hostel to hostel with their alpine-guide T-shirts and their Swiss Army knives and their dreadfully serious faces. Nor could it be said of the two groups at Carter Notch Hut this weekend. One group had fourteen members, the other had ten, and of course they flocked as all such groups will do, mixing neither between groups nor with the rest of us. In my experience, four or five is the limit for the number of people who can travel together and not shut out the rest of the world. I ran a little sociological experiment that morning: I stood at the foot of the path leading down from the bunkhouses and the latrine, and I greeted each person en route to breakfast. Smiles were wasted upon members of the Ten and the Fourteen. They looked away in something like panic, as if they'd been accosted by a midnight cowboy in Times Square. When I realized that smiles would get me nowhere, I changed to a bright "good morning!" Sometimes I had to repeat the offer before it was accepted and returned.

Accepting my isolation, I sat down for breakfast with another solo hiker and four rather elderly ladies. The women had arrived last night between the soup and the main course, having been frightened off the Carter Ridge by the prospect of high winds. They'd spent Friday night at Imp Shelter (which is actually a closed cabin, not a lean-to) and they reported that the wind had blown through the floorboards with such ferocity that their packs had been moved about. So they'd returned to the highway, then climbed to the hut by way of Nineteen Mile Brook Trail. While they were telling this story, I heard a voice behind me, warning off a trespasser: "This is *our* table!"

Them and us, them and us—you can't get away from it, even at Carter Notch Hut.

The wild river country

I had an exaggerated respect for the trail leading south from Carter Notch. I'd traveled it on skis last February, coming up from Jackson to spend a night at the hostel (which, like Zealand Falls Hut, is kept open all winter). Sally was with me. We were the first visitors from the south, at least since the most recent storm, and we soon ran out of tracks to follow. Nor were there any blazes on the trees after we entered the evergreen forest. We were ready to turn back, preferring the known four miles behind us to the unknown mile ahead, when we met a lone skier coming down from

Carter Notch, cutting neat parallel turns between the trees. We followed his track the rest of the way. It was a long mile to the hostel, too steep for us to ski straight up, too narrow for us to sidestep; we had to take off our skis and carry them, floundering knee-deep in snow.

So when I left the hostel Sunday morning, past the bunkhouses and the rock caves, I expected the trail to drop away at a perilous angle. It didn't, of course. Cross-country skis are one thing and waffle-stomper hiking boots are quite another. It was a lovely grade down through the evergreens, and an easy trail to follow now that the snow was off the ground.

Before long I met a middle-aged couple who had a police dog on a very short leash. "We'd appreciate it," said the husband, "if you'd call her 'Bliss.' "

"Hi, Bliss," I said.

The dog checked me out, boots and muddy jeans, and seemed satisfied with what she found. "Thank you," said her master, and took off the leash. "Sometimes she gets upset, meeting people on the trail after we've been out for a few days. She'll be fine now, thanks to your courtesy."

Bliss and her owners had spent the night at a tentsite down the trail, probably the same one Dan Hazen had recommended to the trio with the umbrella tent and the kerosene lanterns. They reported that the trail was dry and easy. I thanked them and said goodbye. Theirs were the last faces I would see on the trail today, at least until I settled myself at Spruce Brook Shelter beside the Wild River, eight miles beyond. I walked generally downhill to the trail junction (where Sally and I had run out of tracks last February) and generally uphill to Perkins Notch, where I lunched at a rather dilapidated lean-to beside a marsh.

This marsh was known as No Ketchum Pond—a lovely name and probably accurate with respect to the fishing, but not at all accurate in a geographical sense. It seems to be a rule in the White Mountains that ponds are known as lakes, and that swamps are known as ponds. I was glad that I would not be spending the night at Perkins Notch. The mosquitoes would have been something to reckon with, or I am no judge of swamps, and the lean-to was in a sorry condition. It was heaped with rubbish and covered with graffiti of a remarkably uninspiring sort. Most of the messages had been written by a laundry marker in a large, looping scrawl: *Ernie and Xxxxx.* The girl's name was different in each case, but Ernie was the author of them all.

From Perkins Notch the trail sloped downhill again, but so gradually that I was seldom aware of the descent. My course was northeast and would remain that way until I left the woods tomorrow. The infant Wild River was on my right, and that too would remain the same. Like most mountain streams it was strewn with boulders, now that summer had brought low water; the river chuckled and gurgled among them, and only rarely did it produce anything resembling a roar. In springtime, though, it is a very different creature—a wild river indeed.

My Pinkham Notch nature walk paid dividends this morning. I could tell spruce from fir, yellow birch from white; I spotted mountain shamrock along the trail, and was gratified when it proved to have a lemon taste that immediately caused my mouth to water. I also recognized a "moss" whose name I had forgotten, but which was not a moss but a compact fern, and which looked like a squad of soldiers marching up a hill, clad in green and bending forward at the hips. (Soldier fern?) The only plant I didn't see, in fact, was hobblebush. No matter; I had replenished my supply of toilet paper at Pinkham Notch Camp.

The day was cool and sunny, a perfect day for walking. And after two weeks on the trail I was in better shape than I had ever been, or probably would ever be. I felt that I could hike forever—that I could set out tomorrow on the Appalachian Trail, two thousand miles from Maine to Georgia. Why not? My knees seemed good for it, and my pack as well. A hike is a hike: you need the same gear for an overnight trip as for a two-week traverse of the White Mountains; what had served me for a fortnight could just as easily serve me for a year. I had my world on my back. According to the scales at Pinkham Notch Camp, it weighed exactly twenty-one pounds.*

I can't remember a happier time that that day on the Wild River Trail. It was even better than the fourth-day high I had experienced on the Garfield Ridge. And the little cloud—the knowledge that my trek would end tomorrow—only added to the pleasure, like the sauce upon the steak I hoped to enjoy at Hastings Plantation. (Gradually, over the past two weeks, I had formed a perfect image of the village at Hastings, Maine. It included a gas station with white clapboard

---

For those interested in such matters, my spare clothing included a wool shirt, wool sweater, down vest, and nylon windbreaker, plus the poncho and a pair of wool socks, weighing in all about five pounds. The sleeping bag and mattress weighed four pounds, the camera one, and the pack itself about three. I was now reduced to less than three pounds of pemmican and orange powder, though that was doubled at the start. I had a red ditty bag for medical supplies (salt tablets, water purifiers, painkillers, gauze pads, adhesive tape, ointment), a blue one for toiletries (tissue, toothbrush, toothpaste, bug repellent, a tube of liquid soap), and a white one for spare parts (polyethylene tent, parachute cord, film, matches, cigarettes). The red and blue bags were stowed in an outside pocket. So were my canteen, flashlight, facecloth, sun hat, jackknife, whistle-compass-matchbox, notebook, today's ration, a few pieces of string, and of course the AMC White Mountain Guide.

siding and the sign of the Flying Red Horse; the pumps were skinny and bottle-necked. Not far away was the Hastings General Store, which also served as the post office and restaurant. The lunch counter was unprepossessing—tired doughnuts beneath a plastic dome—but the steak was juicy, pink, and tender. I don't know why I thought a general-store lunch counter would serve steaks like that, but there it was, and the bill came to something between two and three dollars.) The zest is in the journey and not in the destination . . . but there is nothing like the prospect of journey's end to prompt us to delay and enjoy the scenery.

The trail was dry and untrammeled almost all the way to Spruce Brook Shelter, though with the occasional marshy spot. I saw few bootprints, even where the ground was soft. The Wild River Valley was what hikers expected to find in the Pemigewasset Wilderness: a forest in the process of renewing itself, and almost unvisited by man. I hoped that Congress never attached a wilderness label to this valley. The label would ensure that it was wild no longer. College students would troop in with their kegs of beer, as they commonly did in the Pemi; young lads from Scarsdale would pass the word; and eventually a backcountry patrolman would be dispatched to enforce the limits on overnight camping.

All this may happen anyhow. I am contributing to the possibility, by singing praises to the Wild River in this fashion.

I don't know. Should we hope that backpacking is a fad with only five years of life remaining to it, as the Annual Range Hikers believed? Or should we hope that it will continue to flourish, reaching out from Scarsdale to Roxbury, so that more people can experience its joys?

It is called "the wilderness experience." But it is an experience that is necessarily privileged, because if everybody enjoys it, then nobody does, for the wilderness is wild no more.

There is a thoughtful and lovely essay by Gilbert Hardin describing this process as "the tragedy of the commons." Hardin was concerned about the threat of overpopulation, not the backpacking explosion, but the result is the same: each individual pursues his best interest to the ruin of all. It was once the custom in England to have a common pasture in each community, and this custom was transplanted to the American colonies. (Boston Common was originally such a pasture.) It was a most democratic concept, putting the poor herdsman on the same footing as the wealthy one. This concept still guides the custodians of the White Mountain National Forest. The ghetto dweller can walk the forest if it pleases him, no less than the board chairman of the First National Bank. In the woods we are all equal.

But for every commons there comes a time when it can no longer meet the demands that are placed on it. Each individual may recognize that the commons is being over-grazed, but that doesn't stop him from exploiting it. He alone reaps the profit from his actions; the costs are shared by all. This is true whether we are considering sheep on Boston Common or campers at Desolation Shelter. As Gilbert Hardin described the process:

"The rational herdsman concludes that the only sensible course for him to pursue is to add another animal to his herd. And another; and another. But this is the conclusion reached by each and every rational herdsman sharing a commons. Therein is the tragedy. Each man is locked into a system that compels him to increase his herd without limit—in a world that is limited. Ruin is the destination toward which all men rush, each persuing his own best interest in a society that believes in the freedom of the commons. Freedom in a commons brings ruin to all."

I just don't know. As a solo hiker, I would like to see group hikers banned from the mountains, by persuasion if possible, by fiat if necessary. And almost all hikers are agreed that motorcycles should be banned from the national forest, just as most snowshoers and cross-country skiers are agreed that snowmobiles should be banned. And the shelter bum believes that the AMC hostels are an intrusion, and probably the tenter believes that the lean-tos should go. The end of this logic is that the White Mountain National Forest should be closed altogether. I once suggested exactly that, in a talk at the AMC annual meeting. Needless to say, the proposal was not well received. Yet the logic is persuasive. We must have wilderness at our backs, if we are not to be overwhelmed by the megalopolis that is spreading from Virginia to Maine, paralleling the Appalachian Trail but slightly to the east of it.

We must have wilderness. Not self-guiding nature paths, either, but woods and mountains that a hiker can enter only at some peril, however slight. Without wilderness we shall be less than we once were . . . less than we were in the time of Abel Crawford, less than we were in the days of Joe Dodge and Porky Gulch, less than we were only ten years ago, where I walked three days together on the Garfield Ridge without seeing another hiker.

The White Mountain National Forest cannot survive an infinite expansion in the number of sheep who graze within its boundaries. And the number does seem to have an infinite capacity for expansion. The publisher of this book wouldn't have dreamed of publishing it five years ago, because there wasn't enough interest in the world beyond the pavement. That was before he printed a volume called *Fifty Hikes in the White Mountains,* which sold 12,000 copies in its first two years, and which inspired companion volumes for Vermont, Massachusetts, and Maine. The *AMC White Mountain Guide* is published in editions of 40,000. There are magazines for hikers, too, the glossiest being *Backpacker* with a cover price of $2.50 and a circulation of 110,000. All this since 1972, and of course these publications are bought only by the sensible and the serious. There are legions of hikers who take to the mountains without any guidance whatsoever.

The Great Gulf Wilderness is the wilderness of the future, I suspect. You need a permit before you can enter the Great Gulf; you need a different kind of permit before you can sleep the night, and no more than fifty-nine other individuals can share the experience with you. One of the lean-tos has been torn down; the others are guarded by a caretaker. According to a plan worked out by the Forest Service and the AMC, the remaining lean-tos will probably be demolished soon. Then the Great Gulf will be a preserve for tenters only, sixty of them dispersed through six thousand acres, plus a backcountry patrolman to ensure that they behave themselves.

"What we want to provide," one of the managers had explained to me at Wilderness Incorporated, "is a *variety* of experiences." Thus the Great Gulf will not be a model for the rest of the White Mountains, but only a segment in a jigsaw puzzle of increasing complexity. In other areas, supervised campsites will be the rule, and where a caretaker cannot be justified (at Perkins Notch Shelter, for example) the overnight facilities will probably be abolished. The AMC hostels will remain, of course, for the enjoyment of those who insist upon a salad before the entree, and pudding afterward.

I reached Spruce Brook Shelter about one o'clock. I can't swear to the time, because I was no longer looking at Sally's watch, but had stored it deep in my pack. The lean-to was approached by a foot-bridge over Spruce Brook, with the Wild River still on my right. The bridge had one old handrail and a new one, and on the fresh lumber that fool Ernie had scrawled his name six times.

Ernie had also signed his name to Spruce Brook Shelter, on the Forest Service posters that pleaded "Green Forests Offer More" and "Leave Nothing But Footprints." He was limited to the posters because the shelter was made from boards heavily stained, and his penmanship wouldn't have been legible against the creosote brown. The lean-to, I judged, was no more than three years old. It stood high and dry on concrete footings; its corners were plumb and its roof was without a sag; and the oldest graffiti I could find was dated 1973. It was the neatest lean-to yet, though without the grand outlook or even the character of the older, high-country shelters. I checked the register. Eleven members of the Horton Center Hikers had slept here last night, but of course that was Saturday: I could expect more privacy on a Sunday evening.

Ernie didn't sign the register, by the way. I suppose it was too tame for him.

Hastings plantation   xxi

My first business at Spruce Brook Shelter was to eat another lunch, which I did in splendid solitude. I didn't expect it to last. I was nine miles from Hastings by trail, but for more than half that distance there was a Forest Service road on the south bank of the river, and anyone starting from Wild River Campground could reach the lean-to in a couple of hours. It seemed futile to hope that I would spend my last night alone.

Sure enough, as I was sipping orange-flavored breakfast drink, I heard the *pop-pop-pop* of a two-cycle engine. A trailbike was coming, and I grabbed the camera out of my pack. For two weeks I had been hearing about the menace of motorcycles on the hiking trails, and I meant to photograph this Hell's Angel as he roared past Spruce Brook Shelter. He proved to be a big man on the smallest bike imaginable, closely followed by a boy on a motorcycle of more conventional size. They were father and son from Gorham, N.H., here to fish some beaver ponds they knew about, a few hundred yards up Spruce Brook. Dad had a cigar jammed between his teeth. Cans of Miller High Life were stowed in his pack. He was the prototypical trailbiker—Middle America tooting through the wilderness.

Except that he was more fun than any of the backpackers I had met. He was bluff and easy, and he promised me a couple fine trout for dinner. More immediately, the boy dug into *his* pack and came out with a carton of Devil Dogs—I think I have the right name—a soft chocolate pastry with a ribbon of marshmallow down the center. "Here," he said, pushing one of these cellophane-wrapped confections into my hand. "Here," he said, placing another on my pack: "you can have that one for dinner." Then they settled down to eat Devil Dogs and sip their drinks, Dad with his beer and the boy with a can of Sprite. "Hey!" said the youngster. "Isn't that bag from Sears?" He pointed to my sleeping bag container, which bore the Hillary label that comes with camping gear from Sears, Roebuck & Co. "My dad runs the Sears store in Gorham," he told me, and that was reason enough for us to be friends. They decided to leave their trailbikes in my custody. The boy even wanted to give me the keys, but I persuaded him to take them with him, pleading that I might wander off before he returned.

While we were eating our Devil Dogs, a family of backpackers came up the trail. They looked at the trailbikes but not at us, though they said hello when I did. They kept going, no doubt anxious to leave the Hell's Angels behind them.

We talked about backpackers. "There's too many," Dad agreed, peeling the cellophane from another White Owl cigar. "There's got to be a permit put on them after a while. The Fish and Game has got to find a way to collect some money from those hikers. I read a while ago that the Fish and Game spends fifty thousand dollars a year on search-and-rescue for the hikers, and that money's got to come from somewhere." I had a flash of vision: the lad from Scarsdale obliged to buy a fishing license, to help support the game wardens on their errands of mercy.

I should explain that search-and-rescue is a very big issue in the White Mountains. When a hiker sets out to find the wilderness experience, he does not intend to find so much wilderness that it might endanger his life; if that should happen, he fully expects that somebody will rescue him. And of course somebody does—usually a mixed party of game wardens, AMC personnel, and Forest Service rangers.

Nobody objects to that, and certainly not the lost or injured hiker. But who pays for the rescue party? In Europe there is no argument: the victim is responsible for the full cost of his rescue, even unto a helicopter if one is required to bring him out. Americans take a different attitude toward this matter. Rarely has anyone been presented with a bill for a search-and-rescue party. To hear the Fish and Game department, it bears most of the expense, and that is why the department needs a subsidy from the state legislature. To hear the Appalachian Mountain Club, its crews are the good monks of St. Bernard, and that is why rates are so high at the hostels. . . . The only agency that doesn't complain about the cost of search-and-rescue is the U.S. Forest Service. The USFS operates on a budget devised in Washington, and a Washington budget is not real money. It's only taxes.

While father and son went fishing, I napped on the boulders in the Wild River, waking up from time to time to cool my feet in the stream. The fishermen returned at four o'clock or so. They had three small trout for me. "Do you have any corn meal?" the father asked. I told him no, that I didn't cook on the trail. "Well, do you have any butter, then?" No butter either, and what's more I'd never cleaned a trout. Like a kind teacher with a dull-witted student, he took me down to the water's edge and showed me how and where to open the trout's belly. "Then cut off the head, but don't bother with the tail," he instructed me. "And leave the guts in the brook for other fish to feed on." He watched me clean the second trout, and seemed content with my progress. "You've got to learn to live off the country a little bit," he said. Then he straddled his midget bike, and his son straddled the motorcycle, and they went pop-popping down the trail to Wild River Campground.

When they were out of sight, I realized that they had forgotten their creel. I snatched it up and ran after them, alternately laughing and shouting *hey!* I was overcome by the notion of a hiker chasing two trailbikes along the Wild River.

I caught them, too. "You must be in pretty good shape," the father marveled. Yes, and I'll never be in such good shape again, ninety-one miles behind me, nine miles in front.

I walked back to Spruce Brook Shelter, collecting scraps of birch bark and deadwood as I went along. While my fire burned down to coals, I busied myself with one of those Miller High Life cans. It was the thinnest possible aluminum, and I managed to cut off the ends with my jackknife and then to slice it down one side. It made a passable frying pan. Then I whittled a spatula from a piece of green wood. The trout sizzled nicely without the benefit of corn meal or butter, and only the skin came off when I turned them over to fry on the other side. The flesh turned white and flaky. I ate them one by one, then licked my fingers, the best meal I'd had since leaving home.

Darkness began to gather in the Wild River valley, and I performed
my ritual for the last time. Glasses in one boot; flashlight and bug
repellent in the other; a swallow of water, and so to bed. Nobody had
arrived to share the shelter with me. I fell asleep resolving, if I ever
made another trip like this, to come equipped with a fishing license,
a line, and a hook. The trailbikers had explained it to me: all you had
to do was catch the first fish somehow. After that you could use the
eyes for bait. While it might distress the lad from Scarsdale, wasn't it
all a part of the wilderness experience?

It was raining at dawn, so I went back to sleep until seven. By that
time the rain was so delicate that it scarcely mattered. Anyhow I
wouldn't mind getting wet this morning, because I was leaving the
woods today. I had called Sally Friday night from Pinkham Notch
Camp, to tell her I was on schedule; she would meet me at two o'clock
this afternoon, at the junction of Maine 113 and the Wild River Road.
If I moved smartly, I'd have plenty of time for that steak at the
Hastings General Store & Luncheonette.

Half a mile beyond Spruce Brook Shelter, the main trail crossed to
the south bank on a suspension bridge, which bears the very appro-
priate name of Spider Bridge. It was a spider's web indeed, in the
falling mist of Monday morning. I admired it but did not cross over,
for in that direction lay Wild River Campground and the Forest
Service road. I wanted to delay my encounter with automobiles as
long as possible. So I kept straight ahead on the Highwater Trail,
sometimes fifty feet above the river and sometimes on the level of the
water—which was now wide and deep and full-throated as it rushed
toward its rendezvous with the Androscoggin. This water would
eventually empty into the Atlantic Ocean north of Portland.

The north bank received little traffic, judging by the amount of
grass and shrubbery that grew along the trail. I put on my poncho in
the hope of keeping my legs dry. But the weather inside the poncho
soon became as damp as the grass outside, so I took it off. My jeans
could soak up the dewdrops at their pleasure.

Yesterday I'd passed a county marker, indicating that the Wild
River Trail had taken me briefly into Carroll County. (Oddly enough
there was no second marker, although I had begun the day in Coos
County and likewise ended it there.) That sign gave me a notion that
today I'd be welcomed to the state of Maine. The border crossing
became a small obsession, like the steak that waited for me at
Hastings Plantation, and I entertained myself by imagining the sign
that would celebrate it. My best effort had yellow letters on a brown
field, *NH* on this side and *Maine* on the other, with a vertical line to
show the actual border. It was nailed to a tree, as the county marker
had been.

I never saw the sign. Instead I began to pass half-mile markers, one for *8½ m* and another for *8 m*. This was the trail distance to Hastings, no doubt, and with a certain despair I looked forward to an entire morning of such markers, ticking off the distance like the mileposts on Interstate 93. I needn't have worried. There was no marker for *7½ m*, and my next checkpoint was a natural one, the crossing of Moriah Brook. I sat down with my AMC Guide and determined that I was less than seven miles from Hastings—a much more satisfactory way of settling such questions. In another half-mile, as I reckoned the distance, I heard the sound of automobile traffic above the rush of the Wild River. I was abreast of the campground, though I couldn't see it. All I saw was a small boy fishing the quiet spots among the boulders. I passed without hailing him, not to disturb his dream of solitude.

This was logging country in years gone by, just as the Pemigewasset Wilderness had been, and indeed the whole of the White Mountain National Forest. But the Wild River was at a lower elevation than the East Branch; the trees grew faster here, and it would have taken a woodsman's eye to know that this was second-growth timber. Spruce and yellow birch alike, the trees in many places were two feet thick—large enough to pass for primeval. What I was seeing here was the Pemi as it would be in another generation or two, and again I wondered so many hikers flocked to that region and so few to the Wild River valley.

Now I began to find odd markers along the trail, saplings bent over and flagged with red ribbons, and wedges hammered into the ground. One of the wedges was ominously marked: BASE LINE + 25. Then I spotted a crew of workmen across the river, wearing red hardhats but doing no work that would justify this protection. They were doing no work at all, in fact. I pushed down to the riverbank and hailed them. I had to shout two or three times before they heard me, but then they willingly supplied the information that I wanted. "There's a road going in over there," they told me.

"Along the shore?"

"No, back into the woods. There'll be a bridge across here and a road going back into the woods." The spokesman looked at my pack and walking stick, then laughed with great good humor. Probably he'd discussed this project with hikers before me. "Don't worry," he said. "It won't interfere with the trail."

But how could it not interfere with the trail? I walked back to the red-ribboned saplings, which had set out to become trees but which had now been transformed into something else, flagpoles to honor the highwaymen.

Nine miles is a morning's walk and more, even in relatively flat country. It was after twelve before I spotted the last in that in-

197

terrupted series of mileage markers, this one promising *1 m* to Hastings, and it was nearly one o'clock before I saw the last foot-bridge through the trees. The bridge was a web of cables, like those at Spider Bridge this morning, but it was longer by far. According to the AMC Guide the span was 180 feet, precisely matching that other fine bridge in the Pemigewasset Wilderness, where I had crossed the East Branch in full cry. It swayed and bounced with equal liveliness. On the opposite shore I met a young couple with fishing poles, coming down a stepped path from a parking lot. The boy surveyed my second week's growth of whiskers.

"Come far?" he asked.

If I'd hired him to meet me here with that question, it couldn't have worked out more neatly. "A hundred miles," I told him, with as much pride as I have felt about anything in my life.

The only flaw in this perfect ending was the total absence of the Hastings General Store & Luncheonette. There was no restaurant across the street—no white-clapboard service station—no buildings whatsoever. The town of Hastings existed only as a name upon my map. (As I have since discovered, Hastings was a boom town from 1880 to 1903, while the Wild River valley was cut over; it vanished with the timber that was its reason for being.) I did find a Forest Service sign at a grassy triangle nearby, where the campground road fled away from Maine 113. It told me that this was Hastings Plantation and no mistake, and that sixty-seven acres of spruce were growing here for the enjoyment of future generations.

All right. I would eat the last of my pemmican, fruit and nuts intermingled, and follow it with the last of my orange-flavored breakfast drink. Then I'd sleep away the time that separated me from my two o'clock rendezvous.

But that didn't happen either. Before I picked a spot to lay down my pack—and again as if I'd scripted the ending in advance—the little station wagon rolled into view. Sally had brought along a package of clothes for me. While I changed into them, she laid out a picnic lunch, with a quart of milk to wash it down. Then she produced a thermos of coffee. "Well," she said, *"tell me all about it."* And so I did, drinking coffee in the parking lot at Hastings Plantation.

Notes and sources...

In his *Bibliography of the White Mountains,*
Allen H. Bent marveled about the riches he had
found: "The White Mountains . . . have had
more written about them, probably, than any
other mountains, the Alps alone excepted." Bent
was able to cite 285 books and pamphlets and
about the same number of magazine articles, plus
150 poems and 36 maps—and his bibliography
was published sixty-five years ago. The pace has
quickened since then.

Upon closer inspection, however, these riches
lose much of their glitter. The typical book about

the White Mountains is an entertainment (mine is no exception) and its historical value is therefore questionable. The author is usually content to embroider earlier accounts, showing an understandable preference for the liveliest version; the more imaginative his treatment of the basic anecdote, the better are his chances of being paraphrased in turn. Accordingly, I have tried to go to the earliest possible source, before this process became too far advanced.

A useful exception to the general rule is F. Allen Burt's *The Story of Mount Washington,* published in 1960. It is limited of course to events affecting (or affected by) the highest peak. *New Hampshire: A Guide to the Granite State* was published in 1938 but remains the best New Hampshire guidebook; I have referred to it frequently. It was prepared by the WPA Federal Writers' Project and, among its other virtues, serves to remind us that the government make-work can sometimes have beneficial results. *The Book of the White Mountains,* by John Anderson and Stearns Morse, was published in 1930 and is full of fascinating information, although not everyone agrees on its accuracy. There is no argument about Frederick W. Kilbourne's *Chronicles of the White Mountains,* published in 1916 and still the best history of the region as a whole.

The nineteenth century, especially the last third of it, was the great romantic period in White Mountain literature. Thomas Starr King's *The White Hills: Their Legends, Landscape, and Poetry* (the title itself is romantic) began this outpouring and may stand for all the rest. I have quoted generously from Starr King, like most latter-day authors who want to suggest the beauty of the White Mountains without themselves risking sentimentality. Starr King's epic was published in 1860.

Other useful nineteenth-century sources are *The History of Coos County* (1888), Benjamin G. Willey's *Incidents in White Mountain History* (1856), John H. Spaulding's *Historical Relics of the White Mountains* (1855), and Lucy Crawford's *The History of the White Mountains from the First Settlement of Upper Coos and Pequaket* (1846). The last is not a history, as its title suggests, but an unvarnished tale of the life and hard times of Ethan Allen Crawford. If the White Mountains have inspired a book that will live forever, Lucy Crawford wrote it.

Toward the end of the eighteenth century, Jeremy Belknap completed his three-volume *History of New Hampshire.* References to the White Mountains are scattered through the first two volumes, but the third volume (published in 1792) is especially useful. It is a kind of political and economic geography of the state, including a lengthy section on the White Mountains. Belknap had explored them in person and seems to have been the man who christened Mt. Washington.

In the seventeenth century, John Josselyn wrote the first eye-witness report from the White Mountains. It was published in *New England's Rarities Discovered* (1672), with additional detail in *An Account of Two Voyages to New England* (1674). The authority for Darby Field's ascent of Mt. Washington is Governor Winthrop of Massachusetts Bay, whose journal entry was written in 1642 but not published for a century and a half. Jeremy Belknap, for example, apparently did not read it. He mentions Darby Field's expedition but dates it 1632, and he puts John Josselyn in Field's company, all of which would seem to be erroneous.

Where I have quoted from Winthrop, Josselyn, Belknap, and other early writers, I have sometimes altered the punctuation and capitalization, to avoid puzzling the modern reader. The spelling, however, remains the same.

Appalachia, published twice a year by the Appalachian Mountain Club, is an encyclopedia of information about the White Mountains, though limited for the most part to "exploration," the physical environment, and of course the hiker's world. Its contributors have seldom inquired into such matters as tourism, ski resorts, highways, second-home developments, or (with one notable exception) the logging industry, all of which have changed the backcountry as much as the activities of the AMC. My debts to *Appalachia* are too numerous to list. Three articles were especially useful: Frederick A. Stott's anthology of Joe Dodge lore (June 1974); C. Francis Belcher's history of logging in the Pemigewasset Wilderness (December 1961); and Frank H. Burt's glossary of White Mountain place names (December 1915).

The AMC in recent years has published regular "Bulletin" issues as a supplement to *Appalachia*. These were a valuable source of current information about the White Mountains. Another continuing source was the *New Hampshire Times*. Its signed and unsigned articles (most of the former written by Bill D'Alessandro) kept me up to date on such subjects as Interstate 93, Clivus Multrum toilets, and the Presidential-Dry River Wilderness.

The U.S. Forest Service is engaged in an elaborate effort to catalog the resources of the White Mountains and to chart their future. The first step in this process was a *Guide for Managing the National Forests in New England*, published 1973 in a "Review Draft" and then in final form. Of these, the draft manuscript was more detailed. It was followed in 1974 by the *Forest Plan: White Mountain National Forest*, which narrowed the focus and which likewise was a useful reference. The process is now continuing with the publication of "Unit Plans" for each of twelve geographical regions in the White Mountains. Those for Kilkenny and Kancamagus were published in

1975. Alas, my hike took me through the Kinsman, Pemigewasset, Presidential, and Wild River "units," none of which has yet been inventoried and given its own particular destiny. Had it been otherwise, my speculations about their future would have been more intelligent.

For information about trails and campsites, I have relied on the *AMC White Mountain Guide,* published of course by the Appalachian Mountain Club. The AMC Guide is now in its twenty-first edition. Like a Volkswagen beetle, this volume is improved in small increments, until in the course of years it has become a perfect thing of its kind. No hiker should enter the White Mountains without it.

Finally, I am indebted to several individuals who directed me to sources of information, who were sources themselves, or who checked the manuscript for accuracy. They include Joel White of Pinkham Notch Camp, George Hamilton of the New Hampshire Division of Parks, Daniel Doan (who wrote *Fifty Hikes in the White Mountains*), and especially C. Francis Belcher of the AMC Boston office.

Durham, New Hampshire
March 9, 1976

About the author...

Daniel Ford was born elsewhere in 1931, but soon moved with his family to New Hampshire, which has been his home for more than forty years. He graduated from Brewster Academy in Wolfeboro and the University of New Hampshire in Durham. After a year as a Fulbright scholar in Europe, he served the then-obligatory hitch in the U.S. Army—also in Europe—and later worked as a reporter for The Overseas Weekly.

Ford returned to New Hampshire to try his luck as a novelist. Doubleday published Now Comes Theodora *in 1965. An assignment in South Vietnam provided the material for* Incident at Muc Wa, *published here in 1967 and later in British, Canadian, and Dutch editions. Ford's third novel,* The High Country Illuminator, *was released in 1971, and he is now working on a fourth.*

Between novels, he writes for magazines as various as Backpacker *and* The Nation. *Most of his non-fiction is inspired by the mountains, including the Rockies, the Alps, and his own native Whites, which Ford has been hiking and skiing for fifteen years. He also edits books—notably* The Seasons of New Hampshire *and* Carter's Coast of New England.

Ford lives in Durham with his wife, daughter, and several in-laws, on what he describes as "one of the first communes or one of the last family farms." It is called Shankhassick, after the original name for the river which borders it.